ADVANCE PRAISE for *Playing & Teaching the Saxophone*

"A must-read resource for the band director and studio teacher, for both the beginning player and those serious about current insights into the demands and skills needed to be a well-prepared musician/saxophonist in today's increasingly demanding profession."
—Donald Sinta, Associate Professor Emeritus of Saxophone, University of Michigan

"I love this book! Allison Adams and Brian Horner have authored a wonderful resource. Utilizing innovative organization, it incorporates much-needed essential updates in methodology. It is wonderfully comprehensive, and useful for a variety of circumstances. They have included excellent and interesting diverse musical content, a unique wellness section, and even such details as a 7-week sample syllabus for use in a typical music education methods course. This book demonstrates incredible dedication and investment, and the level of thoroughness and thoughtfulness is impressive."
—Carrie Koffman, Professor of Saxophone, The Hartt School – University of Hartford, Lecturer of Saxophone, Yale University

"This well-organized, seemingly concise, and yet thorough method on saxophone is truly a gem for teachers of saxophonists from diverse levels. The tips and concepts shared within by Dr. Adams and Mr. Horner are spot-on! Keep it near you!"
—Dr. Kenneth Tse, Professor of Saxophone, University of Iowa

"What I find most excellent about this new methods text from Allison Adams and Brian Horner is its balance between approachability and comprehensiveness. Complete with audio and video resources, along with a wealth of other diagrammatic assets, the authors have carefully constructed a complete guide for students and teachers of the saxophone—all while honoring a diverse spectrum of learning styles and environments."
—Kristen McKeon, Product Manager, D'Addario Woodwinds

"KUDOS to Brian Horner and Allison Adams for their wonderful contribution to our music education landscape. DEFINITION is the answer to moving forward in any aspect of life. DEFINITION removes frustrating complications, it amplifies the joy of learning-and-growing, it facilitates mastery in an efficient/effective process. *Playing & Teaching the Saxophone: A Modern Approach*, is a DEFINITIVE BLUEPRINT offering a priceless treasury of benefits to all; PURE GOLD."
—Tim Lautzenheiser, VP of Education, Conn-Selmer Inc.

Playing & Teaching the Saxophone

A MODERN APPROACH

Allison D. Adams and Brian R. Horner

Foreword by Timothy McAllister

OXFORD
UNIVERSITY PRESS

OXFORD
UNIVERSITY PRESS

Oxford University Press is a department of the University of Oxford. It furthers the University's objective of excellence in research, scholarship, and education by publishing worldwide. Oxford is a registered trade mark of Oxford University Press in the UK and certain other countries.

Published in the United States of America by Oxford University Press
198 Madison Avenue, New York, NY 10016, United States of America.

Library of Congress Cataloging-in-Publication Data
Names: Adams, Allison D., author. | Horner, Brian, author.
Title: Playing & teaching the saxophone : a modern approach /
Allison D. Adams and Brian R. Horner.
Other titles: Playing and teaching the saxophone
Description: [1.] | New York : Oxford University Press, 2023. | Includes index. |
Identifiers: LCCN 2022053534 (print) | LCCN 2022053535 (ebook) |
ISBN 9780197627594 (hardback) | ISBN 9780197627600 (paperback) |
ISBN 9780197627624 (epub) | ISBN 9780197627631
Subjects: LCSH: Saxophone—Instruction and study. | Saxophone—Methods. |
LCGFT: Instructional and educational works. | Methods (Music)
Classification: LCC MT500 .A33 2023 (print) | LCC MT500 (ebook) |
DDC 788.7/193—dc23/eng/20221104
LC record available at https://lccn.loc.gov/2022053534
LC ebook record available at https://lccn.loc.gov/2022053535

DOI: 10.1093/oso/9780197627594.001.0001

Paperback printed by Sheridan Books, Inc., United States of America
Hardback printed by Bridgeport National Bindery, Inc., United States of America

Contents

📋 Indicates that the chapter contains a "Hand-It-Over" section available as a PDF download on the companion website; this is designed to be copied and distributed by the band director to students.

🎥 Indicates that demonstration video material for this chapter is available on the companion website. In addition, all tunes throughout the book have been recorded to be used as models.

Foreword

Like other wind instruments, the saxophone has now enjoyed a rich history of textbooks, method books, and manuals designed for both group teaching and private instruction. Within K–12 education it often falls upon the junior high band director or instrumental teacher to impart crucial skills at the earliest, most impressionable period for the student musician. This is a vulnerable time for the young saxophonist when proper fundamentals must be addressed efficiently and effectively. The saxophone suffers from many misconceptions and assumptions by teachers with even the best of intentions, including the often-misguided opinion that "the saxophone is the easiest instrument," a point that fuels the motivations of the authors of this treatise.

This expansive method contains discussion points, descriptions, quick guides, and exercises meant to enhance all levels of instruction and to align the values of early training with the advancing skills of elite high school and collegiate level players. The trickle-down effect that has emerged from ever-increasing demands by composers within advanced wind ensemble music, chamber music, and solo works has brought to light the sheer necessity for equity and access to important information. Saxophone training has truly arrived as a specialized pedagogy apart from all other woodwinds, and this book provides brilliant insight into the steps which will lead any student forward.

Within our profession, we have continued to rely upon some classic methods and manuals which, in some cases, are over a century old. The authors, Dr. Adams and Mr. Horner, have provided a necessary update and major contribution to an ever-evolving pedagogy, while keeping the information fresh and quickly digestible for the modern student. *Playing & Teaching the Saxophone—A Modern Approach* will soon become a staple for any band room or private collection.

Dr. Timothy McAllister
Professor of Saxophone
University of Michigan
Ann Arbor, February 2021

Introduction

The saxophone is notoriously referred to as an instrument that is "easy to play." The truth is that it is easy to play *badly*. The large conical bore of the saxophone makes it a very flexible and responsive instrument. This means that producing a sound is relatively simple, but refining the tone and intonation of that sound takes both guidance and practice.

The first sections of this book—"Getting Started" and "Learning the Notes,"—will take a student in a collegiate methods class or other adult beginner through the fundamental concepts of playing the saxophone. Material will be presented in a way that will allow continuous growth throughout their journey with the instrument. The "In-Depth" section lays out critical concepts that are essential to the further development of any saxophonist. The "Hand-It-Over" sections, indicated in the Contents and available online, are designed to be instructional materials for the students of this book. They are also intended to be used by band directors as handouts for their students. "Teaching Tools" is a quick-reference section that includes guides such as teaching the first saxophone lesson and troubleshooting common problems. These resources, as well as the accompanying video and audio materials, constitute a wealth of educational assets for teachers to use throughout their careers.

This method book not only covers the fundamental sound production and basic fingerings commonly taught to young students, but goes deeper to teach students *from the beginning* how to use their air and tongue position to produce a sound that is resonant and in tune in all registers. Tongue position, often referred to as "voicing" in the saxophone community, is typically taught by saxophone specialists when students advance to the level of private lessons. The result is that students must then uproot bad habits in their playing and relearn fundamental skills the correct way. It is our belief that teaching voicing from the start and developing it alongside other fundamental skills will cultivate young saxophonists who are able to control their tone and play with beautiful sound and intonation.

As a contemporary guide for teaching the music educators of the twenty-first century, this method addresses the pedagogy of not only the instrument, but of the whole student. We have sought to include a diverse array of musical examples to celebrate communities and cultures around the globe. Similarly, a "Wellness for the Young Musician" chapter offers an overview of practices that will help students navigate performance anxiety and avoid injury while playing.

It is our hope that this book provides a method for teaching the saxophone that is specific enough to use as a textbook in a collegiate saxophone methods class, simple enough for a band director to use in guiding their saxophone sections, clear enough for adult beginners to teach themselves the instrument, and deep enough for professionals to use as a resource in teaching private lessons at any level.

📋 Fingering Chart

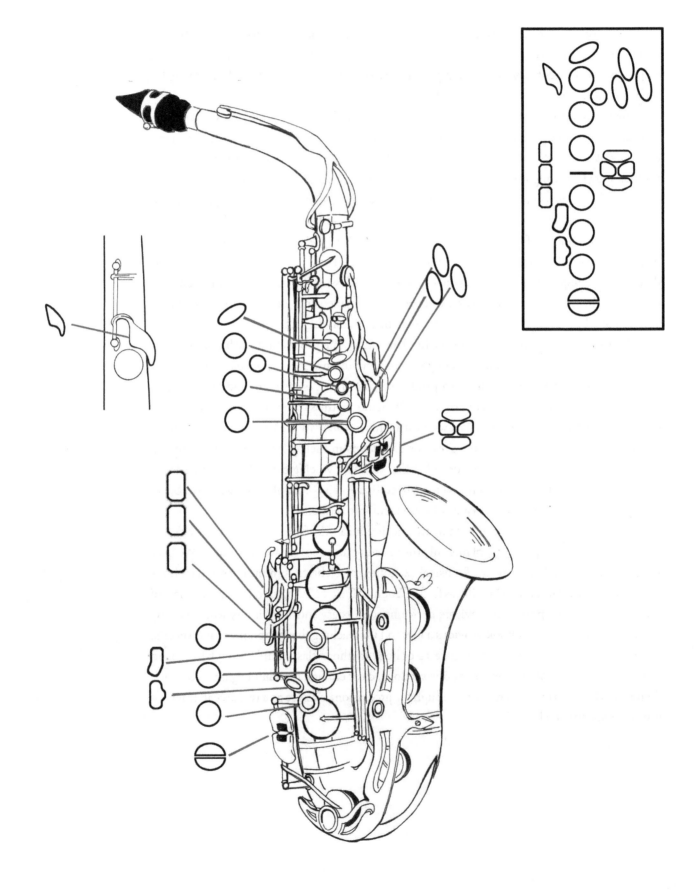

Saxophone Fingering Chart (courtesy of D'Addario Woodwinds)

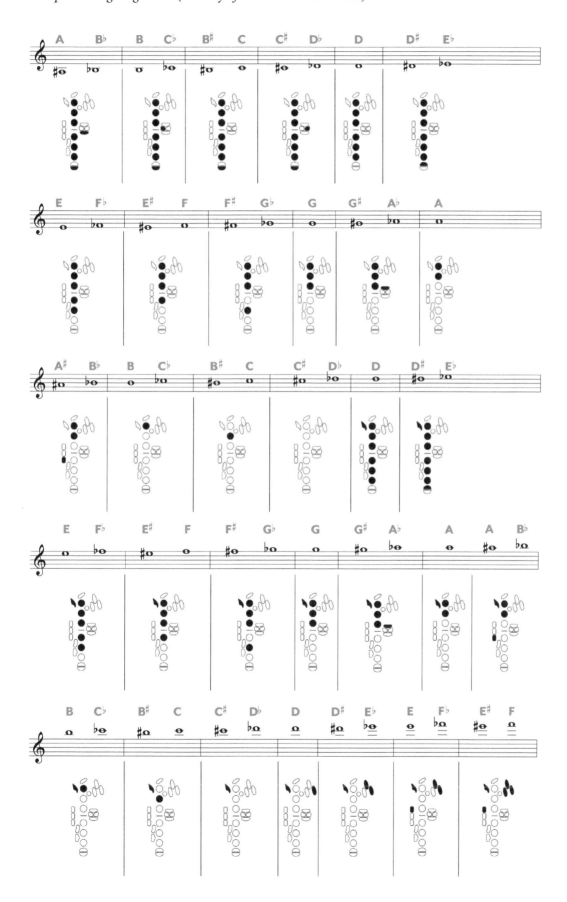

PART 1 Getting Started

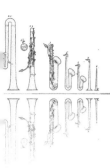

Whether it's John Coltrane's iconic tenor saxophone or Kenny G's straight soprano, the saxophone is one of the world's most beloved instruments. Appearing most commonly as a family of four, including (highest to lowest) soprano, alto, tenor, and baritone, the family includes an additional six instruments that are less well known: sopranissimo (or soprillo), sopranino, C melody, bass, contrabass, and subcontrabass.

Invented in 1838 and patented in 1846 by instrument inventor Adolphe Sax, the saxophone was imagined to be a hybrid of brass and woodwind instruments, embodying the best qualities of each. Its brass body afforded it the strength and power of a brass instrument while its reed and mouthpiece allowed the player to color and shade the tone in the way a flute or clarinet might. Technical advances in its keying system, much of which is shared with the clarinet and flute, solved issues having to do with the covering of holes and positioning of fingers. The result of the improved keywork and responsive conical bore was a unique flexibility that made the saxophone a comparatively easy instrument to play.

The saxophone found an early home in military bands and later achieved fame in the vaudeville era. This led to its role as one of the most recognizable instruments of jazz. Today, it appears in virtually all musical settings, from classical to pop and beyond.

Playing & Teaching the Saxophone. Allison D. Adams and Brian R. Horner, Oxford University Press. © Oxford University Press 2023.
DOI: 10.1093/oso/9780197627594.003.0001

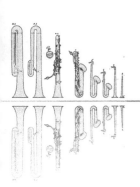

The parts listed below should be provided in the case when a saxophone is purchased or rented. This chapter introduces each part and explains the basic function. For information on upgrading or specific brands, see Chapter 44, "Saxophone Equipment."

Neck Strap

The neck strap supports the weight of the instrument, allowing the hands and fingers to move without holding up the saxophone.

Things to know:

1. The neck strap should always be the first thing a student takes out of the case and puts on.
2. A neck strap with a closed hook is best for a young player. An open hook allows the neck strap to detach from the saxophone, and it can lead to the instrument being dropped.
3. It is important that you have a neck strap with a clasp that you can easily raise and lower. Some are more difficult than others.
4. A saxophone neck strap will come with the instrument, but it is not usually the most comfortable or highest quality strap. When purchasing a new neck strap, it is best to choose one that has some padding, but does not have any elastic bounce in it.

Playing & Teaching the Saxophone. Allison D. Adams and Brian R. Horner, Oxford University Press. © Oxford University Press 2023.
DOI: 10.1093/oso/9780197627594.003.0002

Reed

The reed creates the sound of the saxophone when it vibrates. It is activated by air.

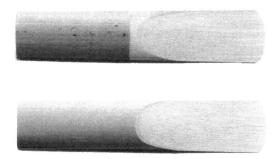

Things to know:

1. Every reed will respond differently, even within the same brand and strength. This is because reeds are made from plants and are always unique.
2. You must be very careful not to touch the tip of the reed. Reeds are very fragile and expensive, and if the tip breaks you need to throw the reed away because the fibers will not vibrate and the sound will be diminished.
3. You should always have three to four reeds in rotation so that if one reed breaks you have another one ready to play!
4. It is very important to soak both ends of the reed before each playing session. You can do this by placing the reed in your mouth while you assemble your instrument, or, preferably, by placing the reed in a cup of water for a few minutes.

You must be sure to *soak both ends*. The fibers of the reed run from top to bottom and it will vibrate better if the entire fiber is wet.

Mouthpiece

The mouthpiece provides a chamber to amplify the vibration of the reed. The reed is placed on the mouthpiece and held on with the ligature.

Things to know:

1. Saxophones usually come with a stock mouthpiece. The mouthpiece is something that should be upgraded after a year or two of playing.

2. The mouthpiece should be stored with the ligature around it, and with the mouthpiece cap over the tip. This protects the mouthpiece from being scratched or damaged in the case.

3. Most players prefer to have a mouthpiece patch on top of the mouthpiece. This thin, inexpensive rubber adhesive (clear or black) makes it more comfortable to rest your top teeth on top of the mouthpiece, as the weight of the head rests here. Mouthpiece patches also protect the top of the mouthpiece from scratches and are sold at local music stores or can be purchased online.

Ligature

The ligature holds the reed in place.

Things to know:

1. Saxophones usually come with a basic metal ligature. The screws will likely be positioned on the bottom side of the mouthpiece, over the reed. Other styles of ligatures may be designed to have the screws positioned on top of the mouthpiece. A good rule of thumb is that the screw handle will always be on the right.

2. The ligature should be stored on the mouthpiece at all times.

3. The ligature can make a big difference in tone production. Professional players will often spend $100–200 on a ligature.

Neck

The neck is the curved part that connects the mouthpiece and the body of the saxophone.

Things to know:

1. There is a cork on the end, and it is very important to keep the cork soft by applying cork grease frequently. This should be done every day when a saxophone is new.

2. Hold the neck so that you are never squeezing any part of the octave vent mechanism that is on the neck. It bends very easily, causing the octave vent to stay open and preventing the saxophone from working properly. If your saxophone makes strange sounds when you blow through it, check that this mechanism is not bent.

Body

The body is the main part of the instrument.

Things to know:

1. When picking up the body, use two hands—one on the bell and the other toward the top. Be very careful not to pick it up by the keys/rods, as they bend easily.
2. On some saxophone models, there is a small rod that sticks up where the neck is attached. Be very careful not to bend this rod.
3. A plastic plug comes with the saxophone, and when the body is in the case, it should always be put in the top opening of the body. This protects the small rod that sometimes protrudes while also ensuring a snug fit in the case.
4. You should swab the body after every practice session.
   a. Place the weight of the swab in the saxophone bell, letting it rest in the curve of the instrument. It is helpful to put the cloth in the bell as well, so that there is enough string to allow the weight to fall through the saxophone.
   b. Gently turn the saxophone upside down so that the weight drops out the smaller end of the saxophone tube.
   c. Carefully pull the string until the swab comes out the smaller end of the saxophone.
   d. Near the top of the instrument, there is a small rod that protrudes into the body of the saxophone. Be very careful that the swab does not get stuck on this rod.

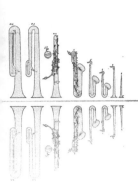

Place the case on the floor or another stable location—be sure the case is right side up! Typically, the case for a beginner saxophone will have the manufacturer's logo on the side that should face up.

Setting Up the Neck, Mouthpiece, Ligature, and Reed

1. Put on the neck strap and cinch the clasp up to the bottom of the collarbone so it will be easy to adjust downward later.
   - Very important! You should always do this first when you put the instrument together!
2. Take out a reed very carefully and soak the thin end in your mouth or in a cup of water.
   - Always have two to three good reeds at a time (four would be best). For now, a "good reed" is one that is clean and is not broken.
   - Never touch the thin tip of the reed. If the tip of the reed breaks, the reed won't work properly.
3. Take out the saxophone neck. Be careful not to apply pressure to the octave vent mechanism.
   - Apply cork grease to the cork on the end of the neck each time you practice.
4. Turn the reed around and soak the thick end in your mouth or in a cup of water.
5. Put the mouthpiece on the neck using gentle twists.
6. Carefully put the reed on the mouthpiece.
   - Hold the reed by the sides (never touching the thin tip).
   - The smooth, flat part of the reed will fit against the flat part on the mouthpiece.
   - Move the ligature up so that there's enough space for the reed to slide under, then slide the thick part of the reed down and through the ligature. The tip of the reed should line up with the tip of the mouthpiece.
   - Be careful to never touch the tip of the reed as it is very fragile.
   - The ligature should be placed over the bark of the reed. Tighten the ligature screws (there may be one or two) just enough to hold the reed securely on the mouthpiece and keep the ligature in place. Be careful not to overtighten or the screws might break.

Playing & Teaching the Saxophone. Allison D. Adams and Brian R. Horner, Oxford University Press. © Oxford University Press 2023.
DOI: 10.1093/oso/9780197627594.003.0003

7. Play on the neck/mouthpiece setup as a warm-up. This allows you to do the following:
   - Check that the reed is lined up and vibrating properly.
     - See Chapter 5, "First Sounds on the Neck/Mouthpiece." If the student cannot produce a sound, start by checking the alignment of the reed on the mouthpiece.
     - On an alto saxophone neck, the pitch produced should be a Concert G♯.
   - Establish good embouchure habits.
     - Working with a small portion of the saxophone allows one to focus on a specific concept without worrying about notes and how to hold the larger instrument.
     - Play several long tones while looking in the mirror, and make sure you are following all the steps to forming a proper embouchure. See Chapter 6, "Embouchure."
   - Observe good posture.
     - Practice sitting or standing with good posture and be sure that the saxophone neck is held parallel to the floor. See Chapter 10, "Saxophone Posture and Hand Position."

Adding the Saxophone Body

1. Set the neck aside in a safe place, being very careful to protect the tip of the reed. If the case is on the floor, kneel to take the body out. Hold the body using one hand on the bell and the other hand on the top of the body. Do not hold it by the keys/rods. Remove the plug from the top of the saxophone body and leave it in the case.
2. Put the neck on the body and tighten the neck screw until snug. Be careful not to overtighten to avoid breaking the screw.
3. IMMEDIATELY hook the neck strap to the saxophone so that you don't drop it!
4. Sit down and check the neck strap height.
   - Let the weight of the instrument be supported by the neck strap, whether between the legs or to the right side of the body (see Chapter 10, "Saxophone Posture and Hand Position" for a more in-depth discussion). When the neck strap is at the correct height, the saxophone mouthpiece will come straight into the mouth. If the instrument is too high or too low, adjust the neck strap so that the player continues to use good posture. They should not need to tip the head up or down to meet the mouthpiece.

Ready to play!

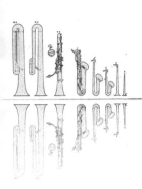

1. If the saxophone case is on the floor, be sure to kneel next to the case.
2. Loosen the neck screw, take off the neck/mouthpiece unit, and place it *in a safe place*.
3. Swab the body.
   - Place the weight of the swab in the saxophone bell, letting it rest in the crook of the instrument. It is helpful to put the cloth in the bell as well, so that there is enough string to allow the weight to fall through the saxophone.
   - Gently turn the saxophone upside down so that the weight drops out the smaller end of the saxophone tube.
   - Carefully pull the string until the swab comes out the smaller end of the saxophone.
   - Near the top of the instrument, there is a small rod that protrudes into the body of the saxophone. Be very careful that the swab does not get stuck on this rod.
4. Place the plug in the hole at the top of the saxophone body.
5. Put the saxophone body in the case.
   - Hold by the bell with one hand, and top of body with other hand.
   - Do not hold the body by the keys/rods.
6. Carefully take the reed off the mouthpiece.
   - Unscrew the ligature and push it up slightly on the mouthpiece to release the reed.
   - Push up on the bottom of the reed or hold the reed by its sides to bring it up and off the mouthpiece.
   - Place reed in its case, being very careful not to break the tip. If the reed tip becomes damaged, it will be difficult to produce sound on the instrument.
     - If using a plastic case with an opening on the side, put the thick part of the reed in before the tip.
   - Place the reed case into the saxophone case. Use a marker or sticker to label the reeds, keeping track of which reeds are in use.
7. Take the neck and mouthpiece apart using gentle twists. Be careful not to put pressure on the octave key mechanism. Place the neck in the saxophone case.

Playing & Teaching the Saxophone. Allison D. Adams and Brian R. Horner, Oxford University Press. © Oxford University Press 2023.
DOI: 10.1093/oso/9780197627594.003.0004

8. Put the mouthpiece cap on and place the mouthpiece/ligature in the saxophone case.

9. Lower the neck strap clasp and take the neck strap off over the head. Place it in the saxophone case.

10. Close and latch the saxophone case. Be sure the case is latched before picking it up, or the saxophone may fall and become damaged.

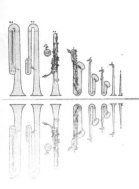

The first sounds should be made on the neck/mouthpiece before putting the entire saxophone together. Articulation should also be taught on the neck/mouthpiece, as outlined in Chapter 9, "AIR-ticulation."

Why?

- It allows you to focus on embouchure, voicing, tone, and articulation without being distracted by fingerings, hand position, and positioning the instrument.
- It allows you to confirm that the reed is positioned correctly and produces a proper sound.
- It helps establish correct playing posture without having to consider the height of the neck strap and the weight of the saxophone.
- Even as you become more advanced, you should continue to play the neck/mouthpiece before putting the neck onto the body. This confirms that the reed is working properly, and that the embouchure/voicing is set.

What Should I Listen For?

The alto neck/mouthpiece together should sound the pitch of Concert G♯. The tenor neck/mouthpiece together should sound the pitch of Concert E.

The chart below outlines the correct concert pitch that should be produced by the neck/mouthpiece combination for alto and tenor saxophone, which are the most common saxophones used by beginner saxophonists.

Producing the correct pitch ensures that embouchure, voicing, and air are working together correctly. See the chapters on those topics for more details.

Playing & Teaching the Saxophone. Allison D. Adams and Brian R. Horner, Oxford University Press. © Oxford University Press 2023.
DOI: 10.1093/oso/9780197627594.003.0005

If the Pitch is Too Low (Common)

- Be sure the saxophone mouthpiece is pushed far enough in on the neck cork. The exact placement varies from instrument to instrument, but the mouthpiece should usually cover about three-quarters of the cork.
- Play using a faster air stream.
- Be sure the back of the tongue is placed in the "hee" position.
- Review the steps to correct embouchure.
- Jaw may be dropped too much.

If the Pitch is Too High (Uncommon)

- Check to make sure the octave key vent is not raised. If the key mechanism has been bent, or if the student is accidently opening the vent by pressing on the other end of the arm, the pad may not be covering the hole on the top of the neck. This will cause the pitch to be about a half step too high.

Refer to the chapters on Embouchure (Chapter 6), Basic Voicing (Chapter 7), and Breathing (Chapter 8) before attempting to create the first sounds on the neck.

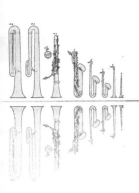

"Embouchure" refers to the muscles of the lips and mouth in the context of how they hold the saxophone mouthpiece. Depending on the style of music being performed, there can be a lot of variation in the embouchure that is taught or observed. For the purposes of this book, we will teach a standard "classical" embouchure, appropriate for a wide range of applications including concert band and solo/chamber repertoire, as well as most jazz band settings. The goal of this type of embouchure is to support the reed while allowing maximum vibration for a fully resonant tone.

The correct embouchure can be formed in three easy steps:

1. Rest the top teeth directly on the top of the mouthpiece so that it supports the weight of the head.
2. Roll approximately one-half of the bottom lip inward and over the bottom teeth.
3. Close the lips around the mouthpiece as if forming a circle. The lips should push in and forward from all directions, as if saying "ooooo" or whistling.

Keep your chin flat, so that the area just below the bottom lip is drawn downward, pulling pressure off the reed and allowing it to vibrate freely. Avoid allowing the chin to bunch upward.

Playing & Teaching the Saxophone. Allison D. Adams and Brian R. Horner, Oxford University Press. © Oxford University Press 2023.
DOI: 10.1093/oso/9780197627594.003.0006

Important Notes About Embouchure

- *Do not let the chin bunch.* This indicates upward pressure on the reed, which will become a major hindrance as the player progresses. To keep the chin flat, the area just below the bottom lip draws downward. This pulls pressure off the reed and allows it to vibrate freely.
- *Do not let the cheeks puff out.* When the cheeks puff out, the corners of the embouchure are not sealing properly, and the air is not directed into the saxophone correctly.
- The purpose of the bottom lip is to cushion the reed. If there is too much pressure applied to the bottom lip as a result of biting upward, the reed will not be able to vibrate freely which will cause a thin tone and sharp intonation (as well as pain in the bottom lip).
- Although you will conceptualize your lips as a circle, it is important to understand that they will not look like a perfect circle because the mouthpiece is not circular.

How Much Mouthpiece Should Be in the Mouth?

When the reed is attached to your mouthpiece, look at it sideways. Hold it up to the light. You'll be able to see where the reed and the mouthpiece meet. This is the fulcrum of the reed, and the spot where your lower lip should rest. The upper teeth should rest on the top of the mouthpiece, directly over that spot.

The Index Card Trick

Use the method below to ensure you are setting up in the right spot. You will need an index card and a pencil.

1. Take an index card and carefully insert it between the reed and mouthpiece.
2. Gently move it down until you feel the spot where it just barely stops. If you let go of the index card here, it may be unstable or teeter, and that's ok. You don't want to push it down too far.
3. Take your pencil and draw a line across the reed that aligns with the bottom of the index card. This is the breakpoint of the reed.
4. Remove the index card.
5. Put your left thumbnail on the pencil line.
6. Insert the mouthpiece until your bottom lip reaches your thumb. This is how much mouthpiece you should take in!
7. Check this spot using your thumb every time you play until you memorize the spot.

Common Mistakes in the Formation of the Embouchure

Bunched Chin

The chin is collapsed upward which allows the bottom lip to push on the reed, dampening the tone and affecting intonation. This is a very common problem with young players and must be corrected immediately. As the player advances, a bunched chin will hinder their progress and become very difficult to change.

"The Smile"

Some older books will instruct the student to turn the corners of the mouth upward into a smile, which is a relic of old-fashioned clarinet playing. This stretches and thins the bottom lip, which dampens the tone by adding unnecessary pressure on the reed.

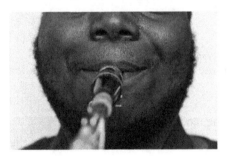

Bottom Lip Protruding Outward

This type of embouchure is sometimes suggested for jazz players because it is conducive to the sub-tone sound commonly used in that idiom. The beginner player will have more control over their lip muscles and resulting tone and intonation if they keep the bottom lip tucked inward. Jazz students may integrate this technique later, once they become more specialized in their training.

Double-lip Embouchure

Although rare, sometimes a student will tuck the top lip around their teeth between the top teeth and the mouthpiece. This can cause a variety of issues and should be avoided entirely.

Jaw Alignment

Students will occasionally push the bottom jaw forward or pull it back. It's important to maintain the natural alignment of the jaw. A dramatic overbite or underbite is not ideal for saxophone embouchure.

The best way to remedy any of these is to review the simple fundamentals of a correct embouchure and model it for the student. Have the student watch themselves in the mirror during each practice session, observing their current embouchure and then correcting it accordingly. Encourage them to also make a mental note of how the correct embouchure *feels*. Although this sounds simple enough, it can be difficult to correct habits that have been ingrained incorrectly. This type of work should be viewed as a long-term exploration, done without expectation of immediate success. The student should not play through any pain or discomfort to create a certain embouchure.

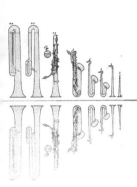

"Voicing" refers to the position of the tongue and the shape of the oral cavity/throat in the context of playing the saxophone. Because changes in the position of the tongue affect the shapes of the oral cavity and throat, voicing instruction throughout this book will be described in terms of altering tongue position.

It is fairly easy to produce a sound on the saxophone, but it is difficult to play with a beautiful, rich tone. If your tongue is not positioned in quite the right spot or your oral cavity is not in the proper shape, you may struggle to find a focused sound and to play in different registers of the instrument.

The study of voicing and the mastery of overtones is a mysterious—and sometimes very frustrating—process. The tongue is one of the most complicated muscles in our body, responsible for many functions from speaking to swallowing to tasting. For most people, these normal functions occur automatically and involuntarily. Mastery of voicing requires us to consciously discover what the tongue must do in this new context and then do it reliably and repetitively. Eventually it will become automatic.

We'll go into greater depth throughout the book, but here are a few voicing basics to get you started.

Tongue Position

There are three parts of your tongue:

1. Back/Base
2. Middle
3. Tip

Default tongue position when playing the saxophone:

- Say "hee"
- Notice how the back of your tongue is raised, with the sides touching the upper back molars. When you play the saxophone, your tongue may not always be in contact with the upper back molars but make this the approximate default position.

Throughout the range of the saxophone, there will be subtle shifts in the default tongue position:

- In the middle range of the instrument, the tongue is in the default "hee" position described in Figure 7.2 (up and back).

Playing & Teaching the Saxophone. Allison D. Adams and Brian R. Horner, Oxford University Press. © Oxford University Press 2023.
DOI: 10.1093/oso/9780197627594.003.0007

Figure 7.1 Relaxed Tongue Position

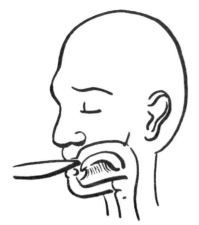

Figure 7.2 "Hee" Tongue Position

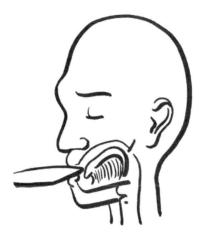

- As the player ascends toward the upper range of the instrument, the arch is exaggerated, and the back of the tongue moves further forward. In this position, the sides of the tongue should be in contact with the inside of the upper back molars.
- As the player descends toward the lower range of the instrument, the arch relaxes somewhat, moving back and down. This feels similar to a yawn in the back of the throat.

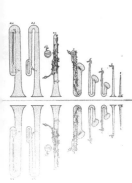

Deep, Relaxed Breaths

Breaths should be deep and as relaxed as possible in any given playing situation. Students should imagine filling their lungs from the bottom up while keeping the torso relaxed, rather than taking a shallow breath that causes the shoulders to rise. As the lungs fill, the stomach should naturally expand.

Put It Into Practice

As an exercise, have students lay on the floor on their backs. Have them place one hand on their stomach and take a deep breath. They should notice that their stomachs go up, and they may also feel their rib cages expanding against the floor beneath them. They should imitate this feeling while playing the saxophone.

Breathing While Playing

1. At the beginning of a piece or when there is enough time:
   - Keep the top teeth anchored on top of the mouthpiece at all times.
   - Lower the jaw slightly and relax the lips to get a good breath, and then form the circular embouchure with the lower lip covering the lower bottom teeth.
2. For a quick breath:
   - Sometimes there is not enough time to lower the jaw to breathe and reset the embouchure.
   - Keep the top teeth anchored on top of the mouthpiece.
   - Relax your lower lip, but keep it in place (covering bottom teeth and resting on the reed).
   - Draw back the corners of the lips and take in air.
   - Resume circular embouchure.

DO NOT allow students to lift their top teeth to breathe!! This disturbs the stability of the horn, and it also puts unwanted pressure from the lower lip onto the reed. Lifting the top teeth to breathe should always be avoided because it will be detrimental to the player's progress.

Playing & Teaching the Saxophone. Allison D. Adams and Brian R. Horner, Oxford University Press. © Oxford University Press 2023.
DOI: 10.1093/oso/9780197627594.003.0008

Learning to Articulate on the Saxophone Neck/Mouthpiece

Articulation on the saxophone has two components: the air that vibrates the reed, and the tongue that defines the start of the sound. The air is critically important and is often underemphasized in the conception and instruction of articulation. Articulation is 80% *air* and 20% *tongue*.

Overview

- The tongue touches the thin end of the reed, or very close to the thin end of the reed.
- Do not use the very tip of the tongue to do this.
- The exact spot on the tongue that touches the reed will vary slightly from person to person. However, a good reference point is about a half-inch back from the tip, on top of the tongue.

Some students will pick up articulation very naturally, and others will have a hard time understanding the correct motion and part of the tongue to use. When teaching, follow the steps below and encourage students to think about how the tongue and oral cavity feel. Ask them to explain what they are experiencing and have an open discussion to help them establish a thorough understanding. Model good articulation for your students and reinforce correct concepts constantly. If a student establishes faulty articulation, it is difficult to change later.

Air

Put your hand on your stomach and say "HA-HA-HA!" Make sure your stomach pulses with each HA.

With round lips, blow out air: "HOO-HOO-HOO." Make sure you are initiating the air with the pulse of your stomach for each "HOO."

Playing & Teaching the Saxophone. Allison D. Adams and Brian R. Horner, Oxford University Press. © Oxford University Press 2023.
DOI: 10.1093/oso/9780197627594.003.0009

We'll use this technique to make the first sound on the saxophone neck/mouthpiece. If you are playing an alto saxophone, the neck/mouthpiece should produce a Concert G♯. If you are playing a tenor saxophone, the neck/mouthpiece should produce a Concert E.

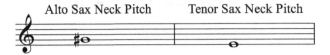

Using the "HOO-HOO-HOO" technique, play Example 1 on the neck/mouthpiece, starting each note with air (no tongue yet). Make sure your stomach pulses with every note.

Troubleshooting

- If the pitch is flat, you may not be supporting with enough air and/or your embouchure may be too loose.
- If the pitch is sharp, you may be using too tight an embouchure. Sometimes this is a result of tucking in too much bottom lip.

Example 1

NOTE: The note G♯ is used throughout this chapter because concert G♯ is the pitch that should sound when playing the alto saxophone mouthpiece and neck without the saxophone body. If the student is on tenor saxophone, the pitch concert E should be used.

Tongue

Part 1: The Motion of the Tongue

Say out loud: "DOOOO DOOOOO DOOOOO."

Notice the motion of your tongue inside your mouth as you say it again. Your tongue starts at the front of your mouth ("D") and moves back and slightly up ("OOOO").

Why so many ooooooo's? You need to follow through with your airstream to support your sound.

"DOO" is the best syllable to imitate as you start using your tongue to start notes on the saxophone.

If you use a syllable like "DAH" or "TAH," you will find that your articulation sounds heavy.

Part 2: The Part of the Tongue that Touches the Reed

Your tongue will strike the very tip of the reed, or very close to the tip. This varies from player to player.

The exact spot on your tongue that hits the reed will vary slightly from person to person as well. A good reference point is that the tongue will touch the reed about a half-inch back from the tip of the tongue. The contact point is always on top of the tongue.

Place your thumb in your mouth, about to the end of your thumbnail. Imagine saying "DOOOOOO" and see if you can find the correct spot on your tongue, touching the tip of your thumb with your tongue.

As described earlier, the back sides of your tongue will be raised, gently touching the upper back molars. This is a good default position as you articulate, but it does not necessarily need to be in constant contact with the upper back molars.

Eighty Percent Air and Twenty Percent Tongue

Play Example 1 on the neck/mouthpiece again, using air to start the sound as you did before ("HOO"). Remember to initiate the air with the pulse of your belly for the start of each note.

Example 1, Part 1 (start sound with air):

Now, with the saxophone mouthpiece in your mouth, say "DOOOOO." When you say the "D" part of the syllable, your tongue should be touching the thin end of the reed, putting just a little pressure on it. When you say "oooooo," the tongue moves back and slightly up. This allows the air to move out of your mouth and across the reed, causing the sound to start. Remember that while the spot on your *tongue* is slightly back from its tip, it will touch near the very end of the *reed*.

Now play Example 1 on the neck/mouthpiece and start each note with the tongue. The start of each note should now sound crisper.

Example 1, Part 2 (start sound with tongue):

DOO vs. TOO

"DOO" should be the syllable used for your default articulation. If you don't hear a crisp start to your note, don't be afraid to use a stronger "D" sound. If you want to accent a note or cause it to stand out even more, try using "Too" instead.

Let's Explore!

Explore the difference in these articulations using Example 2.

Example 2:

Because you are now using air pulses along with the tongue, the start of the note should be crisp, but the ending sound of the note should still sound bouncy. This is an ideal default articulation.

Be sure NOT to use "DOOT" as your default syllable. You don't need to stop the sound with your tongue—the tone will stop when the air stops.

Smoothing Things Out: Legato Tonguing

In Examples 1 and 2, you allowed the air to stop between notes which created a separated, staccato articulation. Sometimes this is the style needed for the music, and sometimes you need a smoother, connected approach.

Example 3: Notice how you use a long, supported air stream to play the long notes in the example below.

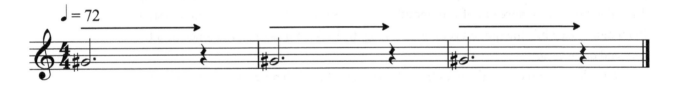

Example 4: Keep the long, supported airstream but now interrupt it with your tongue to create articulated notes that connect to each other. They should no longer sound bouncy.

10

🖺 📹 SAXOPHONE POSTURE AND HAND POSITION

It is crucial that beginning saxophonists establish proper posture and hand position. Because the saxophone uses a neck strap, posture is a bit more complicated than other wind instruments. When students don't use the neck strap properly, it creates problems related to the angle of the mouthpiece, hand tension, and proper embouchure formation. Please read this chapter carefully and establish good habits!

Sitting Posture

Students are usually taught to sit while playing the saxophone, as they will sit during band class and often during group lessons in school.

- Students should sit forward on the edge of the chair, with their backs comfortably straight and feet flat on the floor.
- There are two ways to place the alto saxophone:
  1. To the right side of the lap.
     a. This method is best for smaller students and should be used until they are tall enough to comfortably position the saxophone between their legs.
     b. The keyless side of the instrument should rest on the outside of the right thigh.
  2. In the center of the legs.
     a. This is the preferred method once students are tall enough.
     b. The keyless side of the instrument should rest on the inside of the left thigh.

Playing & Teaching the Saxophone. Allison D. Adams and Brian R. Horner, Oxford University Press. © Oxford University Press 2023.
DOI: 10.1093/oso/9780197627594.003.0010

TO THE RIGHT   CENTER

Note: Tenor and baritone saxophones should always be played to the right side of the lap, not in the center of the legs.

- The saxophone neck strap is a critical component of posture. *The neck strap should support the full weight of the instrument—the saxophone should not be resting on the chair or on the student's leg.* Make sure that the neck strap height is set so that the mouthpiece comes directly to the student's lips as they sit with good posture. The head should not be tilted up or down to reach the mouthpiece.
- Be sure that students do not hold the saxophone out in front of them in a marching band style. This puts pressure on the wrists and fingers and can eventually lead to problems such as carpal tunnel syndrome and tendonitis.

Standing Posture

The standing posture is preferred for solo performances. It affords the player greater mobility and makes it easier to take deep breaths.

- Students should stand up straight with their feet shoulder-width apart, with equal weight on both feet. Because of the asymmetrical weight of the saxophone, it may be helpful to put the left foot slightly in front of the right.
- The saxophone neck strap is a critical component of posture. The neck strap should support the full weight of the instrument. Make sure that the neck strap height is set so that the mouthpiece comes directly to the student's lips as they stand with good posture. The head should not be tilted up or down to reach the mouthpiece.
- Alto saxophone: The E♭ key guard should rest against the student's torso. The exact placement will vary according to height.

- Tenor and Baritone Saxophone: It's often most comfortable for the larger saxophones to be played to the side, with the keyless side of the instrument resting against the outside of the right thigh.
- Be sure that students do not hold the instrument out in front of them and away from their body in a marching band style. This puts pressure on the wrists and fingers and can eventually lead to problems such as carpal tunnel syndrome and tendonitis.

Hand Position

When placing fingers on the pearls, the soft pads of the fingers should contact the pearls. Fingers should be naturally curved and relaxed. As fingers depress the keys, the knuckles of the fingers should not collapse. Encourage students to use light pressure on the keys.

Left Hand on Top

1. Skip the top key, which could be pearl or brass.
2. *Index finger* goes on the next pearl.
3. Skip the small pearl.
4. *Middle finger* goes on the next large pearl.
5. *Ring finger* goes on the next large pearl.
6. *Pinky* relaxes lightly on top pinky key.

7. *Thumb* ON the thumb rest on back (likely black plastic, but possibly brass or pearl).

Approximate thumb placement: the knuckle of the thumb should rest on the outside of the thumb rest, on the opposite side of the octave key.

Right Hand on Bottom

1. There are only three pearls on the lower stack. Place fingers on the pearls in order from top to bottom: *index* finger, *middle* finger, *ring* finger.
2. *Pinky* relaxes lightly on the top pinky key.

3. *Thumb* rests under the thumb hook on the back but it never holds up the weight of the horn. The thumb should be placed so that the pads of the fingers are comfortable on the pearls. This will vary slightly according to hand size.

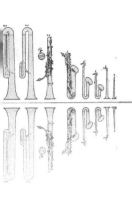

Saxophonists adjust the position of the mouthpiece on the neck cork to arrive at a rough tuning of the instrument. However, a saxophonist will only be able to play all the notes throughout the full range of the instrument in tune if they are also using the correct embouchure, voicing, and reed strength.

Intonation: Mouthpiece Placement

If *overall pitch is sharp*, PULL mouthpiece OUT on the cork. A longer tube produces a lower pitch (Lower, Longer. Get it? Two "L's!").

If *overall pitch is flat*, PUSH mouthpiece IN on the cork. A shorter tube produces a higher pitch.

When tuning, be sure to use plenty of air to produce a full, supported sound, and make sure the tongue is in the correct voicing position ("hee")!

Tune Using Concert B♭

Concert B♭ is often the first pitch used to tune beginning ensembles. This means that an alto/baritone saxophonist would tune their G and a tenor saxophonist would tune their C. These are acceptable tuning pitches for the very beginner, but Concert A is much more reliable and should be the preferred tuning pitch as soon as possible.

Tune Using Concert A

Once a saxophonist has learned the basic notes of the instrument and established good embouchure and air support, they should tune using the notes below. These pitches should be at zero on the tuner and are the pitches that should be used to tune in a large ensemble setting as well. They should hear no "waves" ("wah-wah" sound).

Alto/Baritone Saxophone: Low F♯ and middle F♯ (concert A)

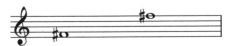

Playing & Teaching the Saxophone. Allison D. Adams and Brian R. Horner, Oxford University Press. © Oxford University Press 2023.
DOI: 10.1093/oso/9780197627594.003.0011

Soprano/Tenor Saxophone: Check middle B (concert A) and also low/middle F♯ (concert E)

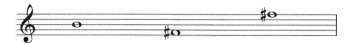

Other Considerations

Temperature

- A cold instrument will play flat. It should be allowed to warm up to room temperature before tuning.
- As a student blows warm air through the instrument the tuning tends to go sharp. This is often the case when a student puts the instrument together, tunes, and then plays before the instrument is warm. Therefore, best results are achieved when a student tunes after playing for a few minutes.

Air/Embouchure

- If a student uses slow air and/or a loose embouchure, the pitch will drift flat.
- If a student uses a tight embouchure, the pitch will be sharp—especially in the upper register.

As a beginning saxophone student, it may be difficult to tune because the embouchure and voicing have not yet become stable. As you work with young students, here are some of the best ways to help them develop correct intonation:

1. Make sure the student can match the correct concert pitch on the neck/mouthpiece alone.

Tips:
- Use your own mouthpiece to test the student's neck and mark the cork with a pencil to show where you can play the pitch in tune.
- Make sure student is using correct embouchure and air support
- Make sure student has the tongue in the "hee" position

2. Play with your students as much as possible to help develop their ear. If the student's pitch is off, assess possible causes (mouthpiece position, voicing, embouchure). However, remember that a student will not have the ability to play consistently in tune until their embouchure is established.

Transposition—What is Concert Pitch?

Concert pitch, also known as concert key, is a common reference that allows communication between members of an ensemble playing differently pitched instruments. For example, you can see below that when the alto saxophone plays a C, it sounds the same as an E♭ on the piano. The piano always plays in concert key.

C on alto saxophone = E♭ on piano

This is often a confusing topic. We'll continue to discuss transposition throughout the book.

🎥 THE SAXOPHONE FAMILY 12

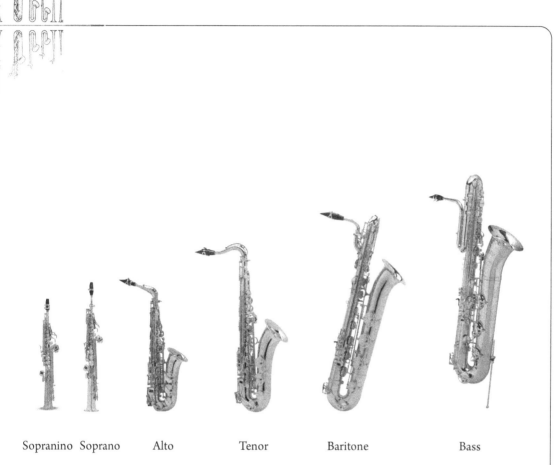

Sopranino	Soprano	Alto	Tenor	Baritone	Bass

Saxophone	Key	Comments
Sopranino	E♭	Rare.
Soprano	B♭	Difficult for high school students to play well.
Alto	E♭	Most standard. Every saxophonist should be proficient on alto.
Tenor	B♭	Uses more air, D and G tend to crack easily so voicing must be adjusted.
Baritone	E♭	Uses more air. Middle D sometimes cracks. Heavy. Have students use a harness-style neck strap when possible.
Bass	B♭	Rare. Used in saxophone ensemble and some band music, such as Grainger.

Playing & Teaching the Saxophone. Allison D. Adams and Brian R. Horner, Oxford University Press. © Oxford University Press 2023.
DOI: 10.1093/oso/9780197627594.003.0012

Doubling Within the Saxophone Family

When students switch between the saxophones, they should check the breakpoint of the reed and mouthpiece (using the index card trick) to make sure they are taking the correct amount of mouthpiece.

The voicing is different for each saxophone. For example, the lower horns require a more open oral cavity. See Chapter 37, "Soprano, Tenor, and Baritone Saxophone," for additional details.

PART 2 Learning the Notes

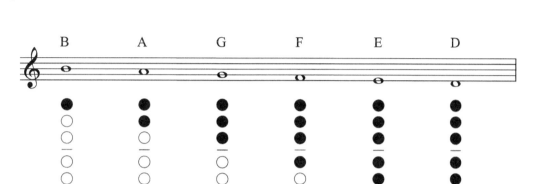

The saxophone is easy! Notice how you just keep adding one finger to play the descending notes above. Many students remember this sequence using the acronym "BAG FED"—like a horse who eats from a bag!

Playing & Teaching the Saxophone. Allison D. Adams and Brian R. Horner, Oxford University Press. © Oxford University Press 2023.
DOI: 10.1093/oso/9780197627594.003.0013

For Review: Hand Position

As fingers depress the keys, the knuckles of the fingers should not collapse. Use light pressure on the keys and develop the habit of keeping your fingers in a naturally curved position.

CORRECT

INCORRECT

Notes in the Left Hand: BAG

Example 1

Example 2

Example 3

Stepping Around!

Example 4

Example 5

Example 6

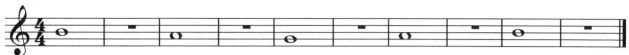

Example 7

Example 8

Keep a long, supported airstream, just like you are slurring, but now interrupt it with your tongue to create articulated notes that connect to each other.

Doo Doo Doo   Doo Doo Doo   Doo Doo Doo   Doo Doo Doo

Let's Play!

Start each note with a tongued articulation but keep your air stream long and connect the notes as much as possible!

Hot Cross Buns

Mary Had A Little Lamb

Au Clair de la Lune

Right Hand Review: FED

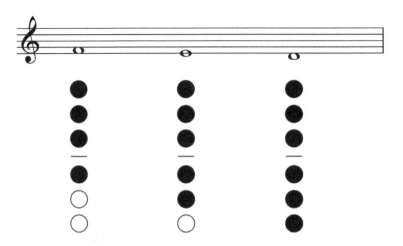

CORRECT   INCORRECT

Example 9

Walking Down to F

Example 10

Walking Down to E

Example 11

Walking Down to D

Example 12

Take a deep, relaxed breath before the start of each phrase and try to produce a full, resonant sound on the low D.

Skipping Around!

Example 13

Example 14

Let's Play!

Three Sad Mice

Let's Explore!

Create a short melody using the six notes that you learned in this chapter and perform it for your friends!

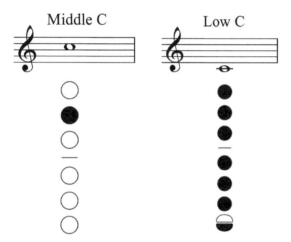

Middle C does not refer to middle C on the piano, but rather the middle C on the saxophone. The saxophone has three Cs in its normal range. We'll refer to them as low C, middle C, and high C (which will be introduced later).

Transposition: The E♭ Alto Saxophone

When a C is played on the alto saxophone, it sounds the same as when an E♭ is played on the piano.

C on alto saxophone = E♭ on piano

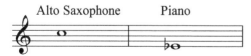

Therefore, the alto saxophone is called the "E♭ alto saxophone."

Playing & Teaching the Saxophone. Allison D. Adams and Brian R. Horner, Oxford University Press. © Oxford University Press 2023.
DOI: 10.1093/oso/9780197627594.003.0014

44

Walking Up and Down: Middle C

When you move your fingers from B to C, you must change fingers quickly so that the transition between these pitches is smooth!

Example 1

Example 2

Example 3

Walking Down to Low C

As you play lower notes, be sure you do not drop the lower jaw. Instead, think of yawning, and let the space inside your mouth get bigger. Your lower jaw and embouchure should stay in their normal position. As mentioned earlier, the arch of your tongue should relax somewhat, moving back and down. Support the sound with lots of air!

Example 4

Example 5

C Major Scale

Let's Play!

Be sure to take deep, supported breaths so that you have enough air to play the low Cs! Experiment with different types of articulation: first use a long, connected articulation, then go back and make everything staccato.

Funga Alafia

Nigerian Folk Song

mf

Pirulito

Brazilian Folk Song

mf

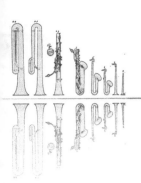

Sometimes it can be difficult to produce an immediate sound on low C. The instrument may not want to speak at all, or a higher pitch may sound. Other than fundamental errors, such as taking too much/not enough mouthpiece into the mouth, incorrect posture, inadequate air support, etc., these challenges have two main causes: leaking pads (particularly located on the low end of the instrument) and improper voicing.

Leaking Pads

Leaks can be confirmed with a leak light (see Chapter 45, "Saxophone Maintenance," for more information). If you suspect a leak, it may be helpful to have a more experienced player try it with their mouthpiece to see if they are able to play the low notes. You may need a trip to the repair shop. If there are leaks, the low notes can be very difficult or impossible to play.

Voicing

If you are producing a higher pitch (or squawk) but your embouchure and air seem correct, you are probably voicing the low C incorrectly. To review, "voicing" refers to the position of the tongue and the resulting shape of the oral cavity and throat, and has a profound effect on the tone, response, and intonation of the saxophone. Here are a couple of general instructions that will help:

- Just like there is a correct position for your hands, there is a correct position for your tongue when you're playing. As described earlier, the position of the tongue while playing saxophone should be UP and BACK, with the back of the tongue making contact with the back molars almost all of the time ("hee").
- The back of the tongue shifts down for the lower notes (a feeling similar to yawning), and higher and more forward for the higher notes.

Playing & Teaching the Saxophone. Allison D. Adams and Brian R. Horner, Oxford University Press. © Oxford University Press 2023.
DOI: 10.1093/oso/9780197627594.003.0015

Introduction to Overtones: The "Low C Squawk"

If you produced a squawking sound when you attempted the low C, congratulations! You have discovered overtones! This is very common and happens to almost all players. The squawk is probably an *overtone* of low C. It is very easy for that low note to jump up one octave if the player does not have their tongue in the correct position.

What Is an Overtone?

Overtones are pitches that are audible above the pitch of the note you're fingering, and they are a result of the physics of the saxophone. When straightened, the saxophone forms a cone. When changes are made to the way that air vibrates within the cone, a predictable series of pitches, or overtones, can be produced.

For example, on C and D the first few overtones that can be produced are shown below:

We've mentioned that the position of the tongue and the resulting shape of the oral cavity is a critical part of playing the saxophone. The most effective way to learn how to manipulate those muscles is through the practice of "overtones." Once you develop the ability to go back and forth between the first overtone and the lower note (called the "fundamental"), it is easier to control low C and the notes below.

How to Produce Overtones

To produce overtones, the tongue must be UP and BACK. We've described this as the default tongue position for playing the saxophone, but the position must be exaggerated to produce an overtone. The student can trick the tongue into the correct position by using the syllable "KOO" to articulate. When articulating using "KOO," the tongue movement at the back of the oral cavity will start the sound rather than the tongue on the reed, and the tongue is forced into the correct position.

1. Play a low D with a "normal" articulation (using the tongue to start the pitch).

Doo

2. Play the low D again with a "normal" tongued articulation, then re-articulate using a "KOO" articulation. Do not add the octave key. If the student successfully produces an overtone, it will almost certainly be a middle D (as opposed to some higher overtone). Some people have to keep trying for days or weeks to make this happen, and others are able to do it instantly. There's a very wide range of "normal" when it comes to overtones!

Close your eyes and pay close attention to what it *feels* like inside your mouth and oral cavity when an overtone pops out, and what it *feels* like when you go back to the fundamental. If you can recognize and reproduce that feeling, you will be able to sustain the overtone and repeat it in the future.

Doo   Koo

3. Go back and forth cleanly. Try for 4 repetitions.

Doo   Koo   Doo   Koo   Doo   Koo   Doo   Koo

Let's Explore!

Continue to experiment with overtones. Find out what is possible on different notes and with different tongue movements, while always paying attention to what it feels like inside the mouth and oral cavity.

By learning to produce overtones, you will become more aware of where the tongue must be positioned to play all the notes of the saxophone successfully and with the best tone and resonance.

Important Notes

1. The "KOO" syllable should be used only in the overtone exercises, and it should never become a method of articulation when playing the saxophone.
2. The octave key should not be used when practicing overtones, but students *should* use the octave key normally the rest of the time.

Application to Low C

Once you have experimented with the overtone exercise on low D, try the same thing on low C. Try to memorize how it feels to produce the low C.

Doo   Koo   Doo   Koo   Doo   Koo   Doo   Koo

Now that you've discovered different voicing positions, see if you can use the lower tongue position to produce the low C more easily.

Low Note Review

1. Allow the back of the tongue to move lower (yawning)
2. Do not lower the jaw or loosen the embouchure
3. Support the sound with plenty of air!

Voicing—Overtone Ping-Pong

Because overtones are more about feeling than reading, we'll leave out the written music. Check out the directions below and then try it with a friend.

- Find a partner. One of you will play the fundamental and the other will play the overtone.
- The first player starts the "volley" by playing a low D (on any of the saxophones, but remember to transpose if necessary to communicate with your partner). The second player responds by playing the first overtone of low D (which is middle D), using the fundamental fingering.
- Continue going back and forth until you've accomplished four clean pairs in which the fundamental note speaks clearly, and the overtone speaks clearly in response.
- Switch roles and repeat until you have another clean volley with four perfect pairs.
- Start again from the top and tackle a different pitch!

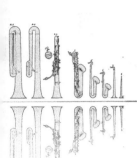

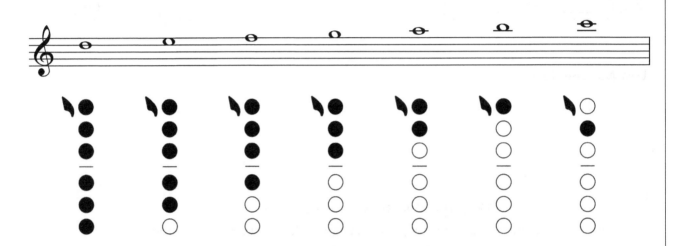

You have already learned the fingerings for low D to middle C. To play the notes above, use the same fingerings, but add the octave key to each one! With this addition of the octave key, you can double the number of notes you know how to play!

The Saxophone Octave Key

As the name implies, the saxophone octave key will change the pitch, raising it by one octave. There are a few important things to remember about the octave key:

- It will be used for all notes starting with middle D.
- The left thumb should rock to depress the octave key.
- The left thumb should always remain grounded on the circular thumb rest—never pick the thumb up.
- On the thumb rest, the thumb knuckle rests on the outside of the circular thumb rest, on the side opposite the octave key.

Playing & Teaching the Saxophone. Allison D. Adams and Brian R. Horner, Oxford University Press. © Oxford University Press 2023.
DOI: 10.1093/oso/9780197627594.003.0016

Correct thumb position for saxophone octave key

Voicing

As you begin to play in the upper register, there are some key voicing concepts to keep in mind:

- Think of the syllable "hee."
- As you go higher in the saxophone range, be sure that the back of your tongue is up and back by the back molars.
- Be careful not to change your embouchure—you don't need to be any tighter with your lips and you don't want to apply upward pressure on the reed. That will result in a thin, pinched sound.

Mechanics of the Octave Key

There are actually two octave vents on the saxophone, both operated by one octave key. The correct vent will automatically open for the fingering played. The lower vent is a very small key that opens near the top of the saxophone body. It opens for D through G♯. The upper vent is located on the top of the saxophone neck. The mechanism that opens it is the metal arm you see. This is the mechanism that students must be careful not to bend when handling the saxophone neck. When the thumb depresses the octave key, the mechanism is activated by the rod at the top of the body, which lifts this arm and opens the vent. It opens for notes above A.

Rocking Back and Forth

Pay close attention to your finger movement and notice the movement of your thumb on and off the octave key. Make your thumb movement as small as possible! You'll notice that it takes practice to coordinate the thumb movement with the addition of all the fingers needed to play middle D.

Moving between middle C and middle D is tricky because of the dramatic change from one finger to many. Also, middle D is the first note to use the octave key, and therefore it requires a shift in voicing. When voiced incorrectly, many students will experience a crack in the sound when going between these notes. Try the voicing suggestions below:

Middle C: "Hee" tongue position (default playing position).

Middle D: Tongue position stays high, but throat is open like a yawn.

Example 1

Example 2

Example 3

Example 4

As you play this example, notice that the octave vent on top of the saxophone neck will open when you play A. It closes for the G because G uses the lower octave vent!

Example 5

Example 6

Scale: C Major

Octave Leaps

Although the octave key is used to change notes, it is also important to think about the tongue position—or voicing—that produces the best tone on each pitch.

- The tongue will generally move up and back to produce the best sound in the upper octave.
- The correct fingering must be paired with the correct voicing to achieve a full, resonant tone on any given note.
- Think about the overtone exercises and the positions that were required of your tongue to play in the low register. Review Chapter 15, "Voicing and Overtones for Low Notes." Use the same voicing now when the low notes appear and note the differences in feel between the high and low notes.

In the example below, use the octave key to change notes, but also use the tongue to help produce the most resonant sound you can in the higher octave.

Example 7

Let's Play!

Bingo

Frere Jacques

The following tune can be played as a round. The first player should start at the beginning. After playing two measures (when they reach #2 on the music), the next player starts at the beginning. When the first player reaches #3 on the music, the third player begins. When the first player reaches #4 on the music, the fourth player begins.

54

Frere Jacques

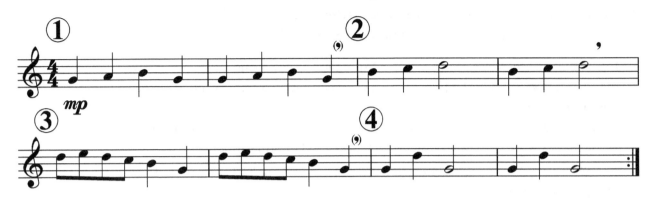

Alouette

Home on the Range

Transposition

Review: Why Is It Called the E♭ Alto Saxophone?

When you play a C on the saxophone, the pitch will match an E♭ on the piano!

Alto Saxophone   Piano

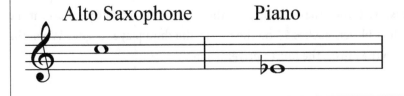

New Note: F♯

Because there is an F♯ in the key signature, all Fs in this line should be played as F♯.

Example 1

Playing & Teaching the Saxophone. Allison D. Adams and Brian R. Horner, Oxford University Press. © Oxford University Press 2023.
DOI: 10.1093/oso/9780197627594.003.0017

56

Example 2

Example 3

Scale: G Major

Example 4

Let's Play!

This tune can be played as a round. The first player should start at the beginning. After playing four measures (when they reach #2 on the music), the next player starts at the beginning.

Sweetly Sings the Donkey

New Note: C♯

Example 5

Example 6

Example 7

Scale: D Major

Example 8

Let's Play!

All Through the Night

New Note: B♭

Example 9

Example 10

Example 11

58

Example 12

Example 13

Scale: F Major

Example 14

Let's Play!

Zum Gali Gali

Hebrew Folk Song

En Harmony

Andante ♩ = c. 80-90

Darius Edwards

Transposition

When you play a C on the saxophone, it will match an E♭ on the piano. That's why it's called the . . . E♭ Alto Saxophone!

   Concert key is a common reference that allows communication between members of an ensemble who are playing instruments that are pitched differently. For example, you can see below that when the alto saxophone plays a C, it sounds the same as an E♭ on the piano. The piano always plays in concert key.

Transposition Challenge 1: Using the staff above as your "decoder," fill in the missing notes below!

   HINT: The saxophone's written note on the staff will always be higher than the piano's written note (concert pitch). Why? That's easy! The saxophone is the best instrument so it's always on the top!!

See Appendix B for answers

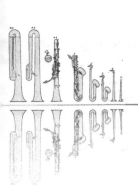

The Flawless Flip

There are two places on the saxophone that are notorious for an audible "blip": between B and C (in both the middle and high octaves) and between F and F♯ (in both the low and middle octaves). In both cases, the "blip" is caused by an imprecise transition from the first finger to the middle finger. Because one finger often raises before the next finger lowers, the note "in the middle" (C♯ in the left hand and G in the right hand) speaks for a fraction of a second, causing the "blip." Slowly practicing an immediate transition will result in a flawless flip!

Play each exercise slurred, then play again tonguing each note. Try playing each line an octave higher as well.

Example 1

Example 2

Playing & Teaching the Saxophone. Allison D. Adams and Brian R. Horner, Oxford University Press. © Oxford University Press 2023.
DOI: 10.1093/oso/9780197627594.003.0018

Daunting D

Another tricky transition is from middle C♯ (all fingers open) to middle D (six fingers plus octave key). This transition has lots of moving parts and requires precise coordination. Furthermore, it requires a shift in voicing or else the tone might crack.

Middle D: Tongue position is high but the throat is open like a yawn
Open C♯: "Hee" tongue position

Be sure to move your fingers together at the exact same time and listen carefully for a clean transition!

Example 3

Sneaky Side B♭

The coordination of fingers can be tricky when playing B♭ using the side key, but you will get used to it with practice!

Example 4

Example 5

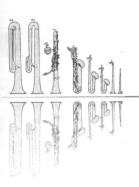

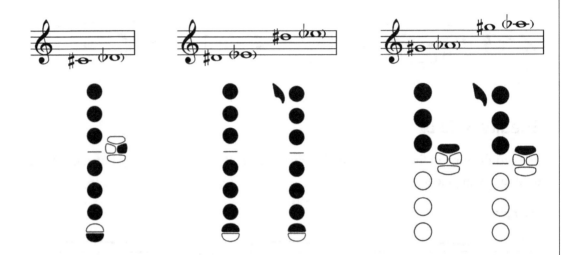

Enharmonics

"Enharmonics" are two notes that share the same pitch, but that are described by different names. They are played using the same fingering. For example, G♯ and A♭ sound the same and are played using the same fingering, but they have different names. They are "enharmonics," or are "enharmonic" to each other.

Left-Hand Pinky Keys

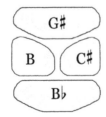

Playing & Teaching the Saxophone. Allison D. Adams and Brian R. Horner, Oxford University Press. © Oxford University Press 2023.
DOI: 10.1093/oso/9780197627594.003.0019

New Note: Low C♯ (or D♭)

<table>
<tr><td colspan="2" align="center">Voicing</td></tr>
<tr><td>Review</td></tr>
<tr><td>Allow the back of the tongue to move lower (a feeling similar to yawning). Support the sound with a lot of air. Do not lower the jaw or loosen the embouchure.</td></tr>
</table>

Example 1

Let's Play!

Piiri Pieni Pyörii

Finnish Folk Song

New Note: D♯ (or E♭)

Example 2

Example 3

Example 4

Scale: B♭ Major

Let's Play!

In the round below, Player 1 starts alone. When they get to Circle 2, the second player joins in. When they get to Circle 3, the third player joins in, etc., until all four parts are being played at the same time!

Shalom Chaverim

Hebrew Round

New Note: G♯ (or A♭)

Example 5

Example 6

Example 7

Scale: A Major

Example 8

Scale: E♭ Major

Example 9

Scale: E Major

Example 10

Scale: A♭ Major

Let's Play!

Plouf Tizen Tizen

Algerian Folk Song

Example 11

Example 12

Example 13

Ho Ho Watanay

Traditional/Iroquois Lullaby

Gle(E)-fully

Allegretto ♩ = 100

Darius Edwards

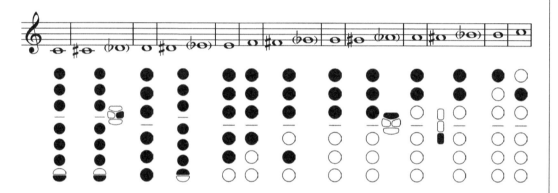

Notes

- There are two notes, F♯ and C, that have special "chromatic fingerings." While these alternate fingerings are useful for avoiding the flip-flop between the index and middle fingers, beginning students should first build a strong technical foundation using the standard fingerings shown above.
- Chromatic fingerings will be discussed in Chapter 25, "Alternate Fingerings," as they shouldn't be taught until late middle school or high school.
- Enharmonics: Chromatic scales are typically written with sharps ascending and flats descending. You've learned C♯ and you'll see it written as D♭; you've learned B♭ and will now see it written as A♯, etc.

Playing & Teaching the Saxophone. Allison D. Adams and Brian R. Horner, Oxford University Press. © Oxford University Press 2023.
DOI: 10.1093/oso/9780197627594.003.0020

Example 1

Example 2

Example 3

Example 4

Example 5

Transposition

The four most common types of saxophone are soprano, alto, tenor, and baritone. These instruments are keyed in B♭ and E♭, alternating as shown below. They all read music in the treble clef, and the fingerings are the same for each type of saxophone. Because they are in different keys, a C on soprano/tenor saxophone is a different concert pitch than a C on alto/baritone saxophone.

- B♭ Soprano Saxophone
- E♭ Alto Saxophone
- B♭ Tenor Saxophone
- E♭ Baritone Saxophone

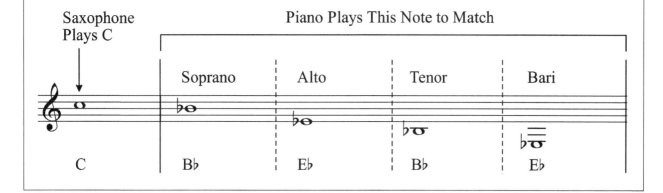

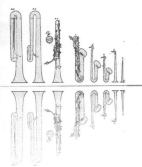

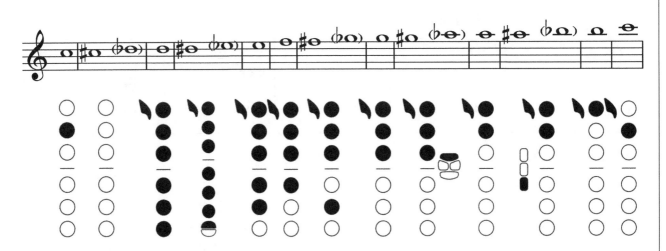

GOOD NEWS: most of this is the same as the lower octave!

Note: Just like in the first octave, there are two notes, F♯ and C, that have special "chromatic fingerings." These alternate fingerings are used to avoid the flip-flop between the index finger and middle finger. They are discussed in Chapter 25, "Alternate Fingerings," and should be taught to students in late middle school and high school. For now, students should build their technical foundation using the standard fingerings shown above.

Example 1

Playing & Teaching the Saxophone. Allison D. Adams and Brian R. Horner, Oxford University Press. © Oxford University Press 2023.
DOI: 10.1093/oso/9780197627594.003.0021

Example 2

Example 3

Example 4

Example 5

One Octave Chromatic Scale (second octave)

Example 6

Two Octave Chromatic Scale

Flawless Fingers Review
When you flip from F to F# or B to C, make sure the motion is coordinated and clean!

Let's Play!

Flight of the (Lethargic) Bumblebee

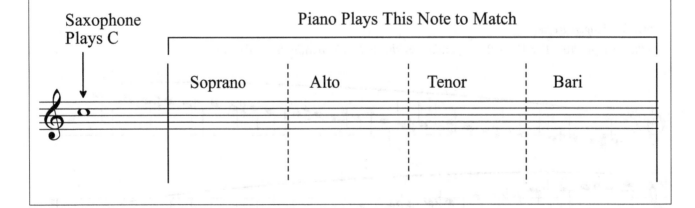

Transposition

In the previous chapter, we discussed transposition for the different members of the saxophone family. See if you can fill in this chart on your own, but look back to check your work.

Saxophone Plays C

Piano Plays This Note to Match

Soprano	Alto	Tenor	Bari

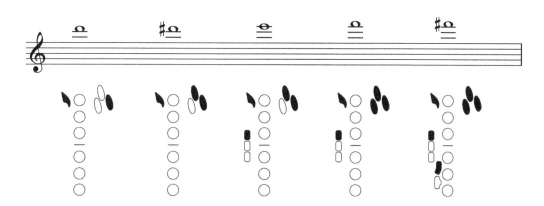

Voicing

Palm Keys: The tongue must be high in the mouth, as if saying "hee." If the embouchure is too tight or if you bite, a thin/pinched sound will be produced, and the intonation will be sharp. If the embouchure is too loose, you lower your jaw, or tongue position is too low, a low/lifeless sound will be produced, and intonation will be flat.

Reed Strength

If you are playing on a 2 or 2.5 strength reed, you may have trouble producing the palm key notes. Difficulty in this register is a sign that it might be time to increase your reed strength. For example, if you are playing on a strength 2.5, try moving up to a strength 3.

Playing & Teaching the Saxophone. Allison D. Adams and Brian R. Horner, Oxford University Press. © Oxford University Press 2023.
DOI: 10.1093/oso/9780197627594.003.0022

Air Support

There's a tendency to be afraid of the high notes. If the palm keys are played with the same amount of air as a lower note, they will "cut through," sounding harsh and shrill. Therefore, many students back off and don't support these notes with enough air. It's important to realize that the palm keys need a confident, gentle approach, paired with the proper voicing and air support. This will take some experimentation to find.

Hand Position

As shown above, you'll add keys as you ascend chromatically.

Palm D: Contact this key near the bottom of the knuckle at the base of the left index finger. You should be close to the fleshy part of the hand, but it is important that you push the key down with the solid part of the knuckle.

Palm D♯: When you add the palm D♯ key, you'll use the same finger (left index finger) as you did for Palm D, but you will contact this key between the base and the first knuckle.

Top right-side key for E: The addition of this key is sometimes confusing to students because it is activated by the right hand. Contact this key at the base of your right index finger, about where your index finger and knuckle meet. This should allow you to keep your hand relaxed and the tip of your index finger pointing down, close to the F pearl. Do not splay your fingers outward.

Palm F: Contact this key near the middle knuckle of the left middle finger. If your hands are large, it may be just below the middle knuckle.

Palm F♯: Add this key with the tip of your right middle finger. Use of the ring finger is also taught; size and shape of the student's hand/fingers can determine which is the best choice.

Example 1

C to D

Be sure you use the correct hand position for Palm D!

Example 2

D to E♭

Is your hand relaxed?

Example 3

C, D, E♭

Try to keep your hand relaxed and your fingers curved! No stiff, straight fingers!

Example 4

D♯ to E

When you play the top right-side key, be sure to use the base of your index finger, close to your knuckle. This should allow you to keep the tip of your index finger close to the F pearl. Establishing this hand position is important so that you can play fast later!

Example 5

D to E

Coordinate the motion of the E palm key and the top right-side key as you go from D to E— they must move together very precisely.

Example 6

E to F

Check your hand position on the Palm F key.

Example 7

D, E, F

Don't forget that you must add two keys for E, one in each hand!

Example 8

Chromatic Movement

Example 9

F to F♯

Example 10

D, E, F♯

Let's Play!

Barcarolle

Jacques Offenbach

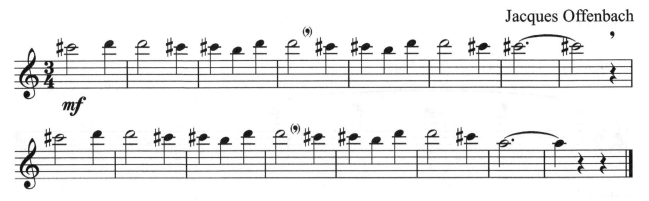

This Old Man

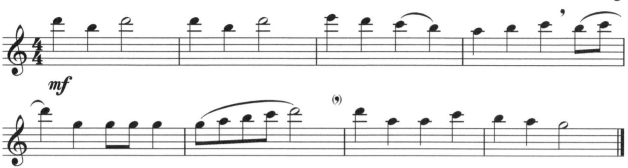

German Dance

Lamb in a High Place

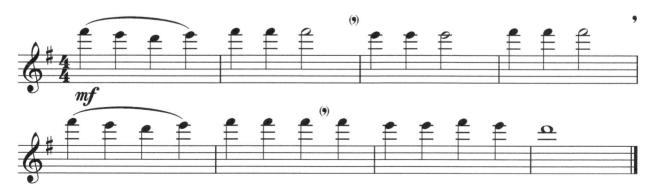

Bb Blues Jam!

Darius Edwards

78

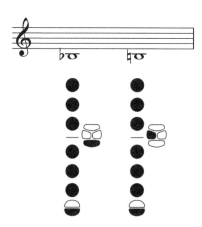

B♭ is the lowest note on the soprano, alto, and tenor saxophone. Baritone saxophones often have an extra key below the left thumb rest, and they are able to play down to low A.

Voicing

Tongue position is low; inside of mouth feels like a yawn.

Do not drop the lower jaw or loosen the embouchure to play these low notes!

You will need a lot of AIR, because the tube of the saxophone is very long with all these keys closed. If you have a lot of trouble with the low register, take your instrument to the repair shop. The lowest pads often leak, making it very difficult to make the saxophone respond!

Playing & Teaching the Saxophone. Allison D. Adams and Brian R. Horner, Oxford University Press. © Oxford University Press 2023.
DOI: 10.1093/oso/9780197627594.003.0023

Left-Hand Pinky Keys

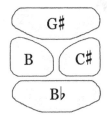

Example 1

Find your low B pinky key before you begin!

Example 2

Find your low B♭ pinky key before you begin!

Example 3

You will need to use a lot of air to start on Low B♭!

Example 4

Example 5

Finger through this example before playing it to review your pinky keys for Low B♭, B, and C♯!

Round in G

Allegretto ♩ = 100

Darius Edwards

Transposition

Fill out the chart, and then use this information to complete the challenge below.

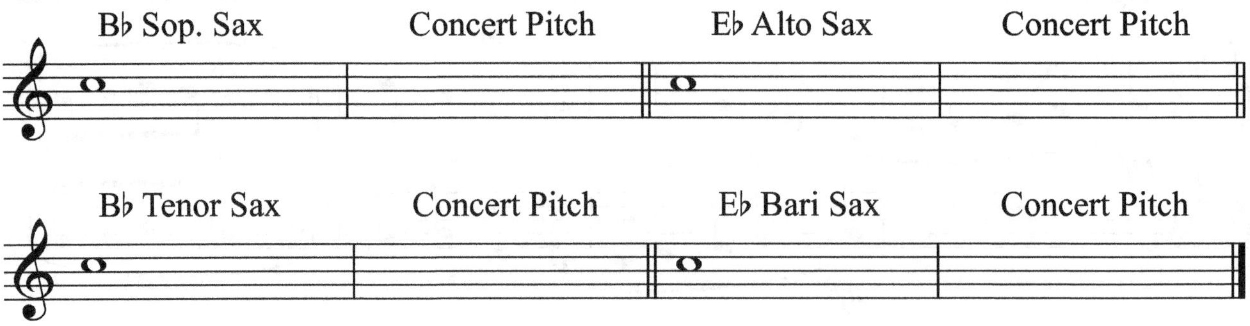

Transposition Challenge 2: As a beginning band teacher, you ask your students to play a Concert B♭ scale. What scale will your saxophone students need to finger to match the rest of the group?

Alto Saxophone: _____

Tenor Saxophone: _____

Baritone Saxophone: _____

See Appendix B for answers

B♭ (A♯) has two common fingerings: "side B♭" and "*bis* B♭." Side B♭ is the first fingering for this pitch that should be taught to beginning students; however, as the student advances they will come across many passages where this fingering can be awkward to use. *Bis* B♭ was added to the saxophone about fifty years after its invention to provide another option—"bis" actually means "twice" in Latin!

To play *bis* B♭, the left-hand index finger slides down to depress both the B pearl and the small pearl below it.

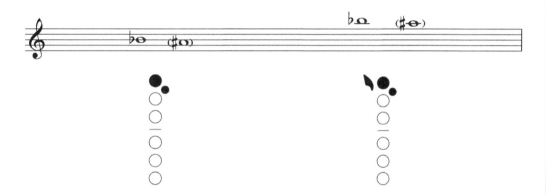

Side B♭ vs. *Bis* B♭: The Do's and Don'ts

Side B♭:

- DO use in chromatic passages.
- DO use for moving between B♭ and C to avoid an unnecessary flip.
- DO use when learning major scales.
- DO (ALWAYS!) use when going between B and B♭.
- DON'T skip learning this because *bis* seems easier.

Playing & Teaching the Saxophone. Allison D. Adams and Brian R. Horner, Oxford University Press. © Oxford University Press 2023.
DOI: 10.1093/oso/9780197627594.003.0024

Bis B♭:

- DO use for most other passages. *Bis* B♭ is usually the easiest fingering choice except when moving to/from a B or C.
- DO use for passages where side B♭ is awkward.
- DO teach *bis* B♭ after the student has a good grasp of side B♭ or when music requires it in late middle school or high school.
- DON'T (EVER!) use *bis* when there is a B♭ next to a B natural—you may not slide on and off the *bis* key between B♭ and B because rolling the index finger onto or off of the *bis* key is not likely to result in a clean transition.
- DON'T let your students use *bis* exclusively. This would violate two of the rules above. Bonus points if you can determine which ones!

In the examples below, the *bis fingering is a better choice than side B♭*. Try each example using *bis* and then side B♭ and see if you agree!

Example 1

Example 2

Example 3

Example 4

Example 5

One-and-One (One-and-Four)

While *one-and-one* is a common fingering for other woodwind instruments, it is rarely used for saxophonists because side B♭ and *bis* provide better technical agility and intonation. However, there are some specialized passages where the *one-and-one* fingering can be useful, such as fast movement between B♭ and F.

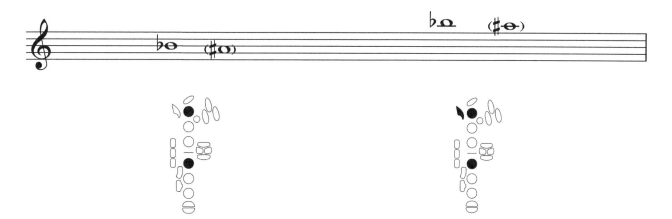

The advantage of using the one-and-one B♭ fingering in the examples below is that the right-hand index finger stays down when moving between notes. This may result in cleaner finger technique. If *bis* is used, the right-hand index finger lifts unnecessarily.

Example 6

Example 7

You'll notice that this example is written in sixteenth notes and is a very difficult passage. This is intended to demonstrate that the one-and-one fingering for B♭ is only used in unusually demanding technical passages with certain characteristics, such as movement between F and B♭. In general, one-and-one B♭ is very rarely the best choice.

Earlier in the book we discussed the importance of the "Flawless Flip"; that is, flipping cleanly from F to F♯ and B to C. There are alternate fingerings that can be used to avoid the "flip flop," and should be used in fast passages, chromatic passages, and trills.

These alternate fingerings should not be taught until all primary fingerings have been established. Students will often start to find these alternate fingerings useful in late middle school and high school.

Alternate F♯   Side C

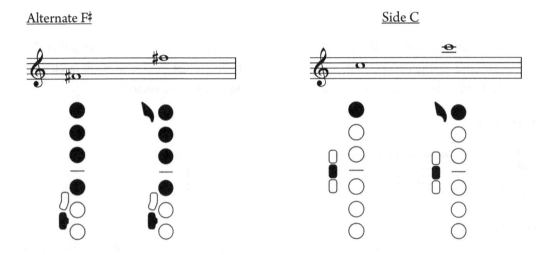

* Sometimes called Fork F♯

Use the tip of the right ring finger to depress on the right index finger, depress the key the alternate F♯ key with the same spot used for the Side B♭ key (between the base of the finger and the first knuckle).

Playing & Teaching the Saxophone. Allison D. Adams and Brian R. Horner, Oxford University Press. © Oxford University Press 2023.
DOI: 10.1093/oso/9780197627594.003.0025

Example 1

This is the same example from the "Flawless Fingerings" chapter. Try it slurred and tongued, with the new alternate fingering for F♯.

Example 2

Use the alternate F♯ fingering for this example.

Example 3

This is the same example from the "Flawless Fingerings" chapter. Try it slurred and tongued, with the new alternate fingering for C.

Example 4

Use side C for this example.

Example 5

Two-Octave Chromatic Scale with Alternate Fingerings

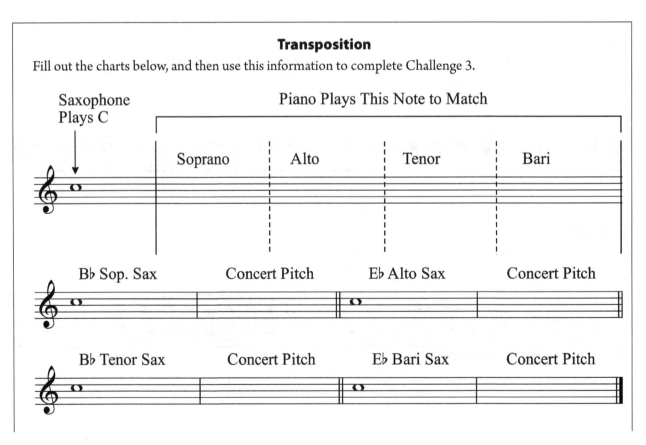

Transposition Challenge 3: As a beginning band teacher, you would like your saxophone students to play Mary Had a Little Lamb together. Unfortunately, you must transpose it for them in order for it to work!

Transpose the first two bars of Mary Had a Little Lamb for your students below so that they are playing the same pitches. Octave differences are ok. Pick a range that would be easy to play for young students.

Concert Key

Alto Sax

Tenor Sax

Bari Sax

See Appendix B for answers

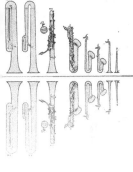

The following composition, "A New Season", was written by Darius Edwards as a capstone performance piece for this method book. Composed for alto saxophone and piano, it can also be performed on tenor saxophone by using the optional part provided. This work showcases the wide range of skills learned throughout this section of the text and could be used as a final playing exam in a collegiate methods class or as a solo work for a younger student. The piano part is intentionally simple so that someone with intermediate piano skills can accompany the soloist.

Please see companion website for a video performance of this work.

Playing & Teaching the Saxophone. Allison D. Adams and Brian R. Horner, Oxford University Press. © Oxford University Press 2023.
DOI: 10.1093/oso/9780197627594.003.0026

Alto Sax

A New Season

Moderato ♩ = 100

Darius Edwards

Alto Sax

Tenor Sax

A New Season
(optional tenor part)

A New Season

PART 3 In-Depth

INTRODUCTION TO IN-DEPTH CONCEPTS 27

Our focus up to this point has been equipping the non-saxophonist music education majors with the basic fingerings and sound production information needed to teach students how to play the saxophone. There are many additional concepts that are critical to musical development, and these will be introduced in this portion of the book. This is also meant to serve as a reference and resource throughout your teaching career, including many "Hand-It-Over" sheets that can be printed out for student use.

Students are individuals and they will progress at different rates. For the student who desires guidance beyond the scope of fundamental band-level playing, this deeper exploration of playing concepts will supplement private instruction or, for a student who may not have access, take its place.

Overview

Chapter 28, "Articulation," covers common problems and exercises to improve articulation.

Chapter 29, "Vibrato," outlines a method for teaching vibrato. Students are often ready to learn vibrato in late middle school to high school.

Chapters 30, 31, and 32, return to a discussion from the first section of this book about how critical voicing and overtones are to tone development. The training presented in these chapters will take a student through the high school years and beyond.

Tuning was covered minimally in the first section because students must first develop proper embouchure and voicing skills. However, once those are established, students must be taught fundamental tuning skills and increase voicing flexibility to find the center of a pitch. This is covered in "Intonation Training" (Chapter 33).

Because reeds are a major component of saxophone tone, it is vital that students understand how to care for them properly. Best practices are discussed in Chapter 34 ("Reed Storage and Adjustment").

Chapter 35, "Developing Musicality," presents insights and exercises to help students transcend the technical aspects of the instrument and move toward realizing its potential for musical expression.

Playing & Teaching the Saxophone. Allison D. Adams and Brian R. Horner, Oxford University Press. © Oxford University Press 2023.
DOI: 10.1093/oso/9780197627594.003.0027

"Introduction to Jazz Concepts" (Chapter 36) discusses how transitioning from the concert band to the jazz ensemble can be a daunting task. This chapter will help!

Although saxophonists often start on alto sax (and sometimes tenor), they will need to have the skills to play other instruments in the saxophone family to fill a concert band or jazz band section. The tips in Chapter 37 ("Soprano, Tenor, and Baritone Saxophone") will help students adapt to various members of the saxophone family.

The altissimo register (Chapter 38) consists of the high notes on the saxophone, above Palm F♯. Young saxophonists are often fascinated with developing this range, and the ever-evolving repertoire for the instrument is demanding these notes at a younger age. This chapter provides tips and exercises for learning to play in the altissimo register.

The saxophone can produce many interesting sounds, and these sounds are being used more and more frequently in contemporary literature, even in concert band music! Chapter 39, "Extended Techniques," gives a short overview of the possibilities.

Articulation is a skill that must be continually refined as a saxophonist matures. This chapter will address common problems, provide articulation exercises, and discuss the advanced concept of double-tonguing.

To review the fundamental approach to articulation, please see Chapter 9, "AIR-ticulation."

Common Problems

1. Concept

Students often think of articulation as the tongue touching the reed. In reality, it is the tongue *coming away* from the reed that allows the tone to sound. Air produces sound and air flows when the tongue moves away from the reed.

2. Point of Contact

On the top side of the tongue, contact occurs about a half-inch back from the tip. On the reed, contact occurs at the thin end of the reed, or very close to it.

3. Motion

Imitate the motion of the syllable "DOO" rather than "TAH."

DOO = tongue moves back and slightly up.
TAH = tongue moves down below reed, which creates a harsh-sounding articulation and
        puts the tongue too low in the oral cavity for optimal tone and intonation.

4. Default Position of Tongue

The back of the tongue should always stay UP and BACK, almost always in contact with the insides of the upper back molars ("hee").

5. How Should a Note Be Stopped?

Default: Use an air release. When you say "DOO," notice how the sound stops when the air stops.

Light Staccato: Start the note with the tongue but use short puffs of air to create a light, bouncy feel.

Playing & Teaching the Saxophone. Allison D. Adams and Brian R. Horner, Oxford University Press. © Oxford University Press 2023.
DOI: 10.1093/oso/9780197627594.003.0028

6. What If I Want a Really Short Note with an Immediate Release?

There are some situations when an abrupt stop to the sound is desirable. This is common in large ensembles when the director wants a clear cut off from the entire group. It can also be needed in rhythmic passages, or in some jazz and rock styles. In that case, you can add definition to the end of the note by stopping it with the tongue, as in "DOOT."

Articulation Exercises

Use this pattern on whatever scale you are currently trying to master to maximize your practice time!

Start by playing the exercises below slowly, working for consistent articulation and note lengths. As you repeat them, increase the tempo and challenge yourself to keep the articulation clean! Play with the metronome to ensure that your tempo stays consistent, and use a steady, supported air stream.

Quarter note equals 60 bpm is a great starting tempo.

Exercise 1

Exercise 2

Exercise 3

Exercise 4

Let's Play!

Exercise 5

This is an articulation exercise based on a tune. Start by playing the example below slowly, working for consistent articulation and note lengths. As you repeat it, increase the tempo and challenge yourself to keep the articulation clean! Play with the metronome to ensure that your tempo stays steady.

A Ram Sam Sam

Moroccan Folk Song

> ### Let's Explore!
> You can also modify a tune by adding repeated notes. While the structure of the melody stays the same, you can work on challenging your ability to articulate (with the added benefit of also working on rhythmic skills and subdividing). Play with a metronome to ensure that your tempo stays consistent, and remember that playing cleanly is more important than playing fast. Speed will come with proper technique and practice. Try playing it up an octave as well!

A Ram Sam Sam Variation

Moroccan Folk Song

Double-Tonguing

Although double-tonguing is a standard skill for many high school flutists and brass players, it is considered an advanced skill for saxophonists (and clarinetists) because having a mouthpiece that enters your mouth makes it more difficult. Saxophonists should focus on developing a fast single tongue in their beginning and high school years. Although double-tonguing should only be developed once a student has reached a very high level, often in college, it can be helpful to understand the concept behind the technique.

Start experimenting with the syllables "DOO" and "GOO," in the following exercises:

Exercise 6

Play this exercise by starting every note with the "GOO" syllable

Exercise 7

The first time, play this exercise by starting every note with the "GOO" syllable. The second time, alternate "DOO, GOO."

Exercise 8

For each beat, use the syllables "DOO, DOO-GOO" for the eighth and two-sixteenth rhythms.

Exercise 9

Continue using the pattern of "DOO, DOO-GOO" for the eighth and two-sixteenth rhythms.

Vibrato is a movement or wavering of pitch that is used to add musical expression. The saxophonist produces this through *movement of the jaw that causes the pitch to vary*. Vibrato has two components: the physical execution and the musical application.

When Should Vibrato Be Taught?

Vibrato should only be taught once a student has a solid grasp of the basic saxophone embouchure and has developed a good overall concept of tone. Ideally, this would happen in late middle school or high school.

The Physical Execution of Vibrato

Place your hand along the side of your face in front of your ear, and with a slow, exaggerated motion say "Vah, Vah, Vah."

Do you feel the motion just in front of your ear?

This is your temporomandibular joint (TMJ). It acts as a sliding hinge and connects the jaw to the skull. When saying "Vah, Vah, Vah," you should feel the ball of the joint shift as your jaw goes down.

Although the motion of the joint won't be this exaggerated when playing vibrato in a musical context, it is important to understand that this is where the motion originates.

Note that the motion of the jaw is straight up and down. It is never horizontally forward into the reed.

There are two slightly different concepts of vibrato that are generally taught in the saxophone community:

1. The sound goes slightly above pitch and then below, with the jaw moving up a little before lowering. In this method, the pitch goes only slightly sharp before dipping flat. If you apply too much upward pressure, it will sound like a "bumblebee buzzing" in the mouthpiece, or it can cut off the sound completely, so be aware that the upward movement is slight. The pitch of saxophone vibrato looks like this:

Playing & Teaching the Saxophone. Allison D. Adams and Brian R. Horner, Oxford University Press. © Oxford University Press 2023.
DOI: 10.1093/oso/9780197627594.003.0029

2. The sound always starts and ends on pitch, and the dips (going flat on the tuner) are created by the lowering of the jaw. The straight line represents zero on the tuner. The pitch of saxophone vibrato looks like this:

Have your student try both concepts and help them assess which produces a better result. You may find some variety among students in which method works best.

Let's Explore!

- Play a middle C and, as you keep your regular embouchure, move the jaw in the exaggerated "vah, vah, vah" motion.
- In Method 1, the jaw moves slightly up, raising the pitch a little, and then moves down, lowering the pitch. In this approach, think about the ratio of movement as 1/3 up and 2/3 down.
- In Method 2, the jaw moves down, lowering the pitch, and then returns to its starting point, the pitch center. You should hear that the pitch gets flat and returns to center as you do this.
- In both methods, the change of pitch occurs when the pressure of the lower lip on the reed temporarily increases as the jaw moves slightly up or decreases as the jaw lowers slightly. This movement is very slight, and must be done with correct embouchure, voicing, and air support to be successful.
- In both methods, it is very important that the pitch always returns to center (does not end in the middle of a vibrato fluctuation), so that it sounds in tune.
- You should also be able to feel that the physical jaw movement is up and down (as opposed to moving horizontally forward into the reed). If you put your hand back up along the side of your face, you may feel a small motion in the TMJ. This exaggerated exercise will help make sure you have the correct basic movement for vibrato.

Exercises for Building Speed

Instead of showing where to tongue, the individual notes in these exercises show how fast the vibrato should go. Do not articulate the notes, but rather make the speed of the vibrato match the rhythm on the page. To do so, use a wider vibrato when the rhythm is slow and allow the vibrato movement to narrow naturally as you increase the speed or subdivision.

You will notice that as you practice this exercise in the higher registers of the saxophone, the pitch is more sensitive to your jaw movements. Therefore, the size of the vibrato wave must be smaller.

Work for even, controlled motion, and make sure that when you end a pitch or change to a new one, you are at pitch, not below or above!

Vibrato Exercise 1

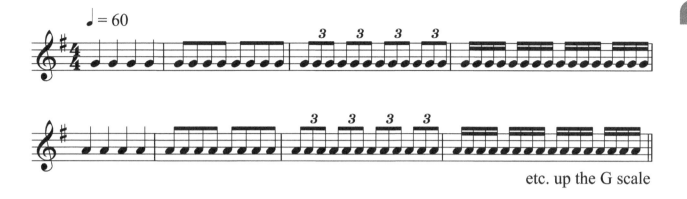

etc. up the G scale

Vibrato Exercise 2

Begin with the metronome set at sixty. When the motion is smooth and even, try out different keys and ranges. Once you have mastered that, increase tempo to sixty-six, then seventy-two, then eighty. If these tempos feel too fast, start slower. It is essential that you master the correct motion before aiming for speed.

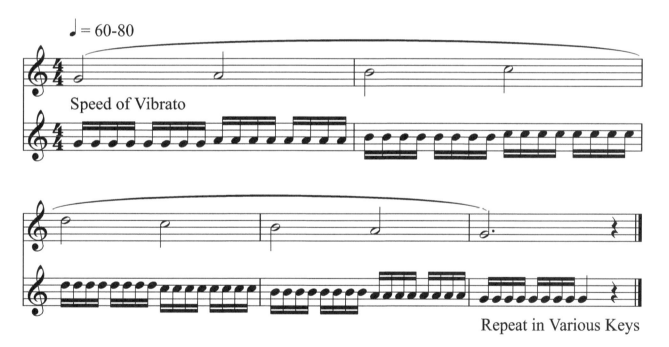

Speed of Vibrato

Repeat in Various Keys

Vibrato Exercise 3

This exercise asks the player to apply vibrato to every other note. This helps you develop the ability to "turn it on and off," but is NOT intended to demonstrate how you will apply vibrato in musical situations.

Try this exercise with the metronome at various speeds. Start by setting the metronome at sixty and increasing slowly in increments of five until you reach eighty. The vibrato movement should be done at the speed of sixteenth notes—four per beat.

Apply this to all of your scales

Apply this to all of your scales

The Musical Application of Vibrato

While the application of vibrato becomes a naturally occurring part of musical expression for the mature saxophonist, it must be studied and intentional at first. The best—and perhaps only—way to learn this is through LISTENING. Identify great musicians whose music moves you and carefully study how they use vibrato. It is good to listen to and imitate professional saxophonists, but it is perhaps even more valuable to listen to and imitate how other instrumentalists use vibrato.

Notice how these musicians don't vibrate on every note and how the speed and width of the vibrato varies. It should NOT be a constant, unchanging presence.

If you listen in a deeply focused and intentional way and work on the exercises below, you'll be well on your way to developing the ability to apply vibrato musically.

The great string players are good examples. There are many, but here are a few to start with:

Violinists: Sarah Chang, Joshua Bell, and Jascha Heifetz
Cellists: Mischa Maisky, Yo-Yo Ma, and Mstislav Rostropovich

Vibrato also has an important expressive role in jazz. Again, there are lots of examples, but here are a few suggestions:

Jazz tenor players: Stan Getz and Dexter Gordon
Jazz alto players: Cannonball Adderley and Charlie Parker

The following exercises will instruct you to add vibrato in an expressive way. Sometimes this is done to emphasize notes that build tension and lead to a resolution, and other times to highlight moments of beauty.

Vibrato Exercise 4

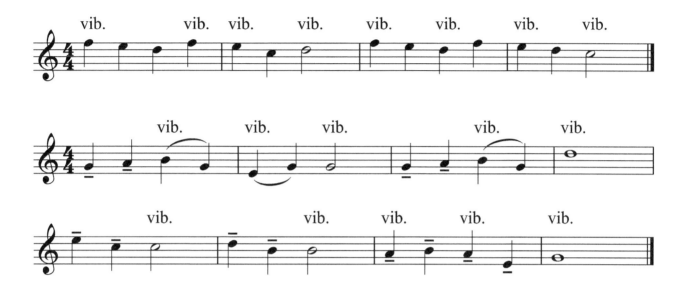

Varying Speed of Vibrato

As you listen to great musicians and apply vibrato to musical examples, you'll find that vibrato has more nuance than simply being "on" or "off." For example, sometimes a player will choose to start the note with a straight tone and increase the speed of vibrato throughout the length of the note. This pairs well with a crescendo. Likewise, musicians will often phase out the vibrato as a note decrescendos and fades away, ending with a straight tone. Try this technique in the example below!

Vibrato Exercise 5

Vibrato Exercise 6

This excerpt is the well-known alto saxophone solo from *Pictures at an Exhibition* by Modest Mussorgsky (orchestrated by Ravel). As you work on this, experiment with different vibrato techniques and applications.

The Old Castle

Modest Mussorgsky

This in-depth section on voicing/overtones will benefit any student who has learned to produce a correct embouchure and has basic fluency on the saxophone. It will include a review of voicing concepts covered briefly earlier in the book. Be sure to work through "Basic Voicing" (Chapter 7) and "Voicing and Overtones for Low Notes" (Chapter 15) before beginning this chapter.

What Is "Voicing"?

"Voicing" refers to the position of your tongue and the shape of your oral cavity/throat, and how they affect the sound you produce on the saxophone. It is one of the most important aspects of playing the saxophone, as it determines the quality and character of your tone and allows you to adjust the intonation of certain notes.

Because the oral cavity and throat are connected, movement of the tongue will change the shape of both. There are varying opinions among saxophonists on where the focus should be placed: whether it should be on the movement of the tongue or the shape of the throat. There's an inherent connection and these principles work together in lowering pitch and finding the ideal resonance for any given note. As students explore voicing, it is easiest to focus on manipulating tongue position to develop control and flexibility of the combined vocal apparatus.

Voicing is the key to eventually producing "altissimo" notes (notes that are above the traditional range of the instrument).

What Are "Overtones"?

On a wind instrument, "overtones" (sometimes called "partials") are notes that make up a predictable series of pitches that can be produced from any given fingering on that instrument. Brass instruments commonly use overtones, as the player must use one fingering to produce several different pitches.

A product of the physics and acoustics of the saxophone's conical bore, overtones are produced when the player changes the way their air enters the instrument, thereby changing the way the air vibrates. The player can make these changes by altering the path of the air as it

Playing & Teaching the Saxophone. Allison D. Adams and Brian R. Horner, Oxford University Press. © Oxford University Press 2023.
DOI: 10.1093/oso/9780197627594.003.0030

Why Should I Care?

The repetitive practice of overtones will:

- Focus and enrich your tone,
- Improve your ability to play in tune,
- Develop your ability to play notes in the altissimo register, and
- Develop the flexibility required to play advanced techniques such as pitch bends.

Overtone Reference Chart

The "fundamental" is the fingered pitch. The overtones are pitches that are created through manipulation of the tongue and oral cavity (fingering does not change).

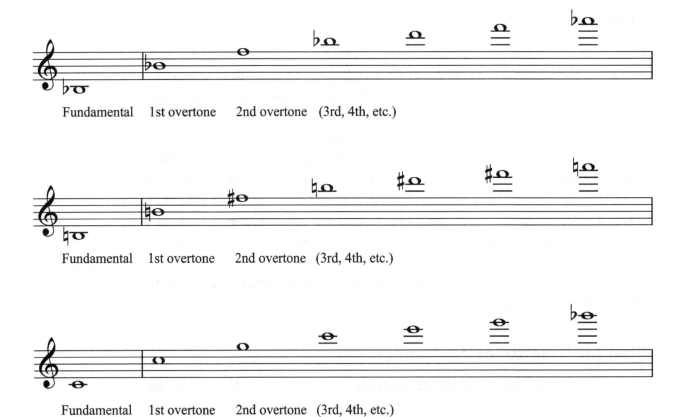

Fundamental   1st overtone   2nd overtone   (3rd, 4th, etc.)

Fundamental   1st overtone   2nd overtone   (3rd, 4th, etc.)

Fundamental   1st overtone   2nd overtone   (3rd, 4th, etc.)

Exploring the First Overtone

Before you progress to more complicated exercises, begin each practice session by warming up with the foundational drills from the Chapter 15, "Voicing and Overtones for Low Notes." They are shown here for your convenience.

1. Play a low D with a "normal" articulation (touching the tongue to the reed to articulate, using the syllable "DOO").

Doo

2. Play the low D again with a "normal" articulation, then re-articulate using a "KOO" articulation (start the sound in the back of the mouth as you do when you say "KOO"). This articulation places your tongue into the correct "voicing position." Do not add the octave key.

Doo   Koo

-   What does it FEEL like when the overtone is activated?
-   What position does it FEEL like your tongue is in?
-   Try to remember that feeling.

3. Go back and forth cleanly. Try for 4 repetitions.

Doo   Koo   Doo   Koo   Doo   Koo   Doo   Koo

Moving Up

This may be easy at first, but it becomes more difficult as you go higher in range.

Let's Play!

See if you can identify this tune and play it using the first overtone! Try this using the "KOO" articulation. Now keep your tongue in the exaggerated overtone position and try it again using the regular "DOO" articulation (starting each note with the tongue).

Moving Up, Part II

Once you are able to play the exercise above, continue up into the higher range of the instrument. This requires practice, exploration of voicing, an exaggerated overtone tongue position, and good air support. Your embouchure should not change.

Let's Play!

See if you can identify this tune and play it using the first overtone! Try this using the "KOO" articulation. Now keep your tongue in the exaggerated overtone position and try it again using the regular "DOO" articulation (starting each note with the tongue).

Let's Explore: Troubleshooting!

In every group that attempts this, there are always some people that struggle—it's totally normal. Here are a few tips that may help:

1. *Trick the saxophone.* Play the overtone you're trying to produce with its regular fingering, then slur to the fundamental fingering and try to maintain the sounding pitch. For example, if you're trying to produce a first overtone from low C:
   - Play middle C and, without stopping the note or re-articulating, close the rest of your fingers to play the low C fingering.
   - Try to make the middle C pitch (which is now the first overtone of low C) continue. It may continue for a second or two, then "fall." Think about how it felt during the time the overtone came out—try again and concentrate on that feeling and see if you can maintain the overtone a bit longer.
   - Or, if you're trying to produce a first overtone of low F, play middle F with the octave key and, without re-articulating, release the octave key.
   - Try to maintain the higher pitch (which is now the first overtone of low F). As above, it may continue for a second or two, then "fall." Think about how it felt and try to replicate it.

2. *Get ugly.* You may not be exaggerating the tongue position enough. Take everything we've discussed in this chapter and do it MORE. Re-articulate HARSHLY using the "KOO" syllable. Forget about quality of tone and focus on making your tongue position more extreme—jam the tongue UP and BACK. Enjoy this—you'll have to reign it back in once you produce some overtones and learn what it feels like. It's not often you'll get to play ugly on purpose!

3. *Experiment with Syllables.* As you get more comfortable with the tongue position needed to produce these overtones, you may find that the syllable "hee" also works well in starting the sound of the overtone. For some players, the syllable "KOO" causes the back of the tongue to move too much as the sound of the overtone begins and "hee" may help keep the voicing position more stable.

Moving Down

For the low notes below, remember to allow your tongue to move down into the "yawn" position.

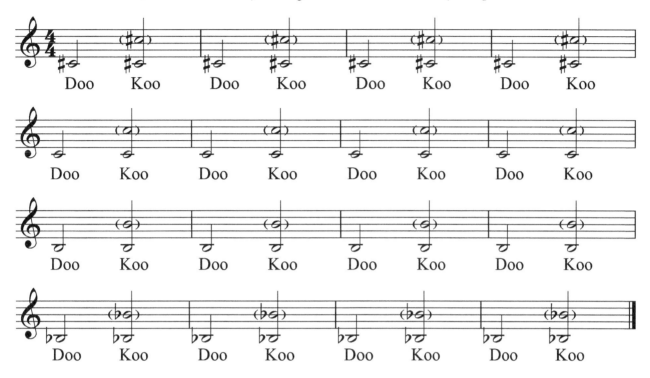

Low B♭ is often the most difficult note to master for this exercise. If you are having trouble isolating the first overtone of low B♭, this exercise should help!

Mix It Up!

Now that you've explored isolating overtones in the exercises above, let's use them to play a short melody. Remember that you will finger the bottom notes, but then use your voicing to produce the upper pitches.

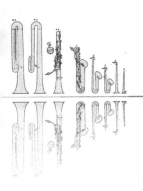

31

VOICING AND OVERTONES: THE SECOND OVERTONE

The second overtone is the next pitch in the natural overtone series (see the chart at the beginning of Chapter 30). On the saxophone, it is a twelfth (an octave plus a fifth) above the fundamental. It is produced in much the same way as the first overtone, but the movement of the tongue and oral cavity are exaggerated.

Voicing Review

- As you start the second overtone, say "KOO" and concentrate on what your tongue does at the beginning, during the "k" part of the syllable. It automatically moves UP and BACK to make this sound.
- Immediately after the "k" sound is released, the arch of the tongue comes forward slightly, allowing air to pass out of the mouth during the "oo" portion of the syllable.

The extent to which the back part of the tongue is positioned up and back will depend on the note you're playing—a decision you'll begin to make automatically as a result of the awareness and mastery you'll develop through ROVR, the Repetitive Overtone Voicing Routine suggested later in the book.

Playing & Teaching the Saxophone. Allison D. Adams and Brian R. Horner, Oxford University Press. © Oxford University Press 2023.
DOI: 10.1093/oso/9780197627594.003.0031

Exploring the Second Overtone

- Finger the notes that are not in parentheses.
- As you change fingerings to the low note, the audible pitch should always stay in the upper register.
- The pitch should continuously match the first note in each line, although there will be slight changes in tuning.

The first three lines of this exercise are usually very easy to master. However, the voicing becomes more difficult as the exercise ascends. It is normal for a student to "get stuck" around G♯ or A, and it will take time to find the correct voicing to go higher.

Starting from the Bottom

To produce the second overtone, use the syllable "KOO" and be sure to support your sound with air.

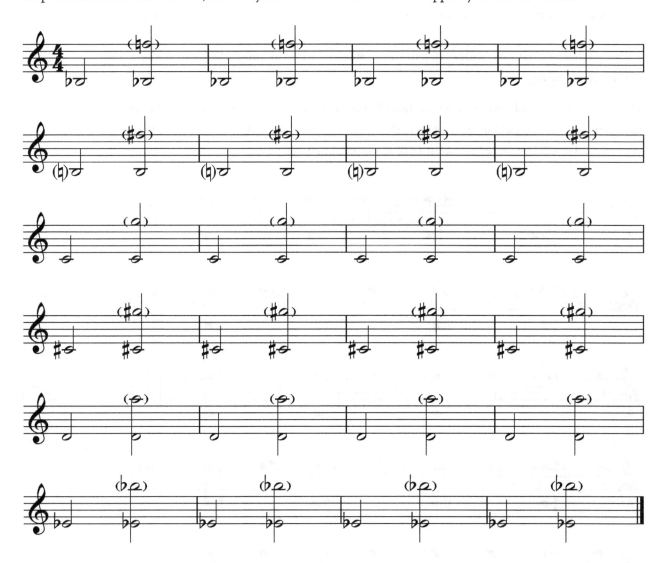

Mix It Up!

Try this using the "KOO" articulation. Now keep your tongue in the exaggerated overtone position and try it again using the regular "DOO" articulation (starting each note with the tongue).

Combining the First and Second Overtones

F = fundamental

1 = first overtone (octave)

2 = second overtone (octave plus fifth)

Keep going! Ascend chromatically as far as you're able!

Let's Play!

The Tired Tongue Blues

How Do I Use Voicing in Everyday Playing?

As you practice overtones, you are learning that each note has not only a correct fingering, but also a particular tongue position that allows that note to have full resonance. Therefore, once the player has mastered the tongue positions and oral cavity shapes involved in playing overtones, it's important to keep the tongue in a "voiced position" while playing.

This means constantly and actively involving the tongue in tone production by moving it along a smooth continuum of positions from the low end to the high end of the instrument as you play. When you later apply this to a musical excerpt or scale, your tongue will move along this continuum throughout the range of the instrument without your conscious involvement.

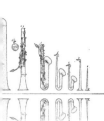

▣ ▣ OVERTONE PRACTICE ROUTINE: ROVR 32

The Repetitive Overtone Voicing Routine (ROVR), combines the exercises in the previous two chapters into a routine that should be part of a daily warm-up. The exercises are not written out—having seen them earlier, focus now on the internal movements of your throat and tongue without the distraction of reading music. Although the focus is on overtones, it is equally important to make sure that the fundamental notes speak clearly as well. After all, it's a *voicing* routine and proper voicing is what allows the proper production of the lower notes too. The routine calls for four repetitions so that true mastery is developed. You'll discover that producing an overtone once and producing it four (perfectly clean!) times in a row are two very different endeavors!

F = fundamental
1 = first overtone (octave)
2 = second overtone (octave plus fifth)
3 = third overtone (two octaves above fundamental)

- Begin on low B♭. If the overtone on this pitch is too difficult, begin on the lowest note that produces a responsive overtone; however, continue to work on these problematic pitches.
- Play four perfect repetitions using the syllable "KOO" to start the overtone.
- Move up one chromatic pitch and perform four perfect repetitions. Continue to ascend until you can no longer produce a first overtone (strive to reach middle C♯).

1. F → 1 (4x)

   Begin on low B♭. Ascend chromatically as high as possible.

2. F → 2 (4x)
   1 → 2 (4x)

   Begin on low B♭. Ascend chromatically as high as possible.

Playing & Teaching the Saxophone. Allison D. Adams and Brian R. Horner, Oxford University Press. © Oxford University Press 2023.
DOI: 10.1093/oso/9780197627594.003.0032

3. Optional integration of the third overtone:

  $F \rightarrow 3 \ (4x)$

  $1 \rightarrow 3 \ (4x)$

  $2 \rightarrow 3 \ (4x)$

Begin on low B♭. Ascend chromatically as high as possible.

Although the best initial tuning pitches on any saxophone are its low and middle F♯, it is also very helpful to tune middle B. Because middle B has a natural tendency to be lower, checking this pitch helps ensure that you will not be flat. Sometimes students will work diligently to place their F♯ in tune without realizing that they are doing so with improper air support and voicing. They will pull the mouthpiece out too far to compensate, which can result in playing flat overall. Eventually, you will be able to tune both F♯ and B and they'll match as an intonation checkpoint. In the meantime, strive for as much agreement as possible, and understand that it is better to be a little sharp than to be flat because this is easily corrected through voicing.

In an ensemble setting, all saxophone players should be encouraged to check their F♯ and middle B against the Concert A tuning note. Checking fourths and fifths in addition to unison pitches is a very helpful tuning technique. The specific processes outlined below can be done in ensemble tuning, or in individual practice against a drone pitch while looking at a tuner.

Alto/Baritone Saxophone (E♭ Instruments)

1. Tune Concert A pitches: low F♯ and middle F♯.
2. Check the pitch of middle B to make sure it is not flat. If it is flat, push in.
3. Play the F♯s against the tuner to check them again. If they are now very sharp, correct voicing/embouchure/air is not being used.

Playing & Teaching the Saxophone. Allison D. Adams and Brian R. Horner, Oxford University Press. © Oxford University Press 2023.
DOI: 10.1093/oso/9780197627594.003.0033

Soprano/Tenor Saxophone (B♭ Instruments)

1. Tune Concert A pitch: middle B.
2. As middle B is a slightly flat note inherently, it's also very important to tune low/middle F♯. Even when tuning in a group, F♯ (Concert E) will sound fine because it is the fifth of concert A.
3. If the mouthpiece is pushed in too much to accommodate middle B, it is likely that the F♯ pitches (and the instrument in general) will be sharp.

Correcting Intonation After Tuning

Tuning the notes listed above will put the saxophone mouthpiece in the best position for good overall intonation. Beyond that, you must compensate for tuning tendencies on specific pitches because of the inevitable acoustical compromises that manufacturers make in the placement of tone holes. You'll create this compromise through the use of voicing, while maintaining proper air support and embouchure.

As a general suggestion, pitch can be lowered by pushing the arch of the tongue slightly forward (see the discussion on "Mouthpiece Flexibility" later in this chapter) and/or by creating space in the throat or larynx while the tongue stays in the "hee" position. Because the tongue and throat are connected, movement of the tongue will change the shape of the throat, and changes in the shape of the throat will result in tongue movement. There are varying opinions among saxophonists on where the focus should be placed when lowering pitch: whether it should be on the movement of the tongue or the shape of throat. We believe there's an inherent connection and that these principles work together in lowering pitch and finding the ideal resonance for any given note.

When pitch is flat, check that the tongue is in the "hee" position, embouchure is not too loose, and correct air support is being used. If all those components are in place, the only way to raise a pitch is by opening another key as a vent.

See "Saxophone Pitch Tendency Guide" (Chapter 43) for a reference list of notes that are typically sharp/flat on the saxophone and quick tips for correction.

Mouthpiece Exercises

Mouthpiece Pitch Check

When played alone with the correct embouchure, voicing, and air support for classical and concert band playing, the mouthpiece should produce the following concert pitches:

Soprano Sax   Alto Sax   Tenor Sax   Baritone Sax

Troubleshooting

If the mouthpiece pitch is too high:

- You may be biting (pushing lower lip up into the reed).
- Embouchure may be too tight.
- The back of the tongue may be too high or too far back.
- You may not be supporting with enough air.

If the mouthpiece pitch is too low:

- The back of the tongue may be too low or too far forward.
- Embouchure may be too loose.

If there is unsteady sound:

- Air support may be inadequate.
- Air stream may be unsteady.

If there is a pinched sound:

- There may be too little mouthpiece and/or too tight embouchure.

Mouthpiece Flexibility

Once you can consistently produce the correct pitch on the mouthpiece, flexibility can be developed by using the tongue and oral cavity to bend the pitch downward. This is done by positioning the tongue in the default "hee" position and then pushing the arch of the tongue forward. It is crucial that any pitch movement be accomplished through voicing, and not by releasing embouchure pressure or lowering the jaw. The technique of lowering the jaw is used only for the production of vibrato.

Be sure to hold the mouthpiece so that it enters the mouth at the same angle that it would if it were attached to the saxophone. At first, the pitch movement will be minimal. With practice and increased tongue manipulation, you will be able to bend the pitch down a half step, and eventually a third or more. A professional player has a range of about an octave on the mouthpiece alone. This skill takes repetition and perseverance.

The musical notation below shows concert pitches used for the alto saxophone mouthpiece. The same exercises can be repeated on soprano, tenor, or baritone saxophone. Refer to the mouthpiece pitches previously listed for each instrument. Practice these bends at a piano, matching each pitch as you go.

Let's Explore!

Once you have mastery of a major third, challenge yourself to play a simple three-note tune such as *Mary Had a Little Lamb* on the mouthpiece.

1. Slide between each pitch.
2. Use air to start each pitch, leaving a short separation between each note. Listen carefully to the start of the sound. Is it steady and on pitch?
3. Articulate each note with the tongue. Make sure every note starts on pitch.

Mary Had a Little Lamb

Traditional

Voicing

Pitch-bending on the mouthpiece cultivates an automatic reaction of the tongue and oral cavity that will result in the ability to play the instrument in tune. This helps to combat notes on the saxophone that are inherently out of tune. For example, middle D on any saxophone tends to be significantly sharp. Once you have mastered pitch bends on the mouthpiece, you'll be able to immediately execute the tongue position that must be paired with the fingering for "D" to play the note in tune.

Playing with a Drone Pitch

A *drone pitch* is simply a sustained pitch. Many tuners and tuner apps have the capability to produce drones, and a quick search of the internet will provide you with many options.

Practicing with a drone pitch will improve your ear and help you learn to match intonation by listening rather than by watching a tuner. After all, we listen to music with our ears, not our eyes!

As you work with a drone, it is important to understand a few important principles of playing in tune. Many students think that every note should register on zero when looking at a tuner, but this does not account for our traditional system of "just intonation." This is a system of intonation in which musical pitches are tuned in relation to one another. For example, when the tonic pitch is in tune, a major third should register fourteen cents flat in order to *sound* in tune. A minor third must be sixteen cents sharps to *sound* in tune. A perfect fifth needs to be just a bit sharp (two cents). In contrast, pianos are tuned in "equal temperament," which is a system that makes small compromises across the keyboard so that the notes sound *as in tune as possible* in every key area.

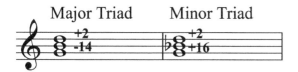

How to Practice with a Drone Pitch

1. Unison notes

Start a drone pitch and sustain a matching pitch on the saxophone. Intentionally drop the pitch flat and try to hear the waves or "wah-wah" effect, which sounds almost like a steady beating of your sound against the drone. Bring the pitch back up to the drone's pitch. You should hear the pitch lock into place and resonate as you find the optimal spot. If you are playing a note that easily goes sharp, repeat this exercise on the sharp side.

2. Scales

Put the drone on a pitch and play that pitch's major scale very slowly. Listen to each pitch and make sure the interval is in tune. Make sure it is fully resonant and that you don't hear any "beats." You could also use minor scales, triads, thirds, etc. In the beginning, you may find it helpful to put a visual tuner on your stand to confirm if a pitch is sharp, flat, or in tune. However, as you develop your ear, you should rely more on the sound and less on the visual device.

3. Repertoire

In a piece of tonal music, put the drone on tonic and play the melody slowly. Listen carefully to make sure all intervals are in tune.

4. Warm-ups

Simple warm-up exercises with a drone pitch are a great way to start any practice session.

These are often based on scales and triads, but they may combine these notes in various ways.

Example 1

Put the drone on tonic (Concert B♭ for alto/bari or Concert F for soprano/tenor) and play slowly, listening carefully for each interval to be in tune.

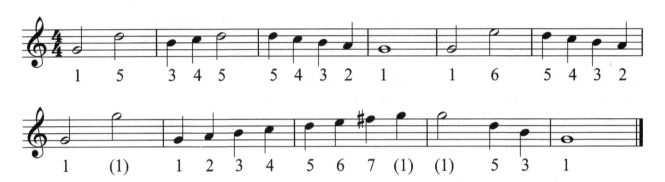

Example 2: Tuning Major and Minor Triads

Remember that you must tune intervals according to the system of just intonation, as shown above. Play very slowly and listen carefully to the placement of each pitch.

Drone Pitch for Alto/Bari: E♭
Drone Pitch for Soprano/Tenor: B♭
If you want to change this into an example with minor triads, change the E's to E♭'s.

Drone Pitch for Alto/Bari: E

Drone Pitch for Soprano/Tenor: B

If you want to change this into an example with minor triads, change the E♯'s to E naturals.

Drone Pitch for Alto/Bari: F

Drone Pitch for Soprano/Tenor: C

If you want to change this into an example with minor triads, change the F♯'s to F naturals.

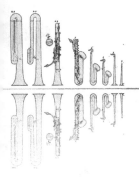

Put nicely, reeds can be tricky. In fact, it seems that the more advanced a player gets, the pickier they are about their sound, and the more troublesome reeds can be. Reeds are made from cane, and as a natural product there are inherent differences from reed to reed. Consistency is the most prized attribute of a group of reeds and saxophonists will have varied opinions on which manufacturers make the most consistent reeds. We both play and endorse D'Addario Woodwinds reeds and feel that the consistency is unmatched. However, as we've mentioned, there are very high quality and high consistency reeds available from several other manufacturers.

We'll explore three ways to cultivate consistency in your reeds:

1. A storage system that provides a flat surface with consistent levels of humidity and temperature.
2. A routine for breaking in reeds and determining their characteristics once stabilized.
3. Making very minor adjustments to the position and surface of the reed.

Reed Storage

Proper storage for reeds will allow them to stay perfectly flat and to be exposed to a constant level of humidity and temperature. Some players use a Tupperware container with a digital humidity meter and reeds held onto pieces of plexiglass with rubber bands, while others use store-bought reed containers, such as the D'Addario Woodwinds Reed Storage Humidification System (which includes a humidity control pack) or Vandoren's Hygro Reed Case. The ideal humidity in a reed case is about 72%.

Playing & Teaching the Saxophone. Allison D. Adams and Brian R. Horner, Oxford University Press. © Oxford University Press 2023.
DOI: 10.1093/oso/9780197627594.003.0034

Reed Stabilization Routine

Players develop their own routines for breaking in and selecting reeds, but most will rotate a small number of reeds and will break them in slowly over a period of days. Here's a sample routine:

Day 1

1. Open five reeds and mark their cases with the date and a number (1-5).
2. Soak the reeds in water for three to five minutes.
3. Play each reed for fifteen to thirty seconds in the middle register of the saxophone at a mezzo-piano or mezzo-forte dynamic.
4. Let the reed dry, flat side up, for about ten minutes.
5. Store each reed and keep these five together so you can identify them as a set.

Day 2

1. Soak the reeds in water for one to two minutes.
2. Play each reed for about two minutes in the middle register of the saxophone at a mezzo-piano or mezzo-forte dynamic. It is good to play long tones, scales, simple melodies, etc.
3. Let the reed dry, flat side up, for about ten minutes.
4. Store each reed and keep these five together so you can identify them as a set.

Days 3–7

1. Soak reed #1 for two to three minutes. Play reed #1 while you put reed #2 in to soak.
2. Play each reed for about the following amount of time:
   a. Day 3: Three minutes
   b. Day 4: Five minutes
   c. Day 5: Seven minutes
   d. Day 6: Ten minutes
   e. Day 7: Fifteen minutes
3. On Day 7, if a reed still feels and/or sounds bad, experiment with reed adjustment or discard the reed.

After this point, practice on the first reed in the set for about twenty minutes. When finished, continue practicing with the next reed in the set. This will maintain a consistent rotation of reeds. Professional players will rotate several reeds through a single practice session to maintain a healthy supply of performance-ready reeds.

As the reeds stabilize, keep notes about the performance of each reed. For example, use a star if the reed feels great, or perhaps adjectives like stuffy, soft, bright, dark, etc.

Simple Minimally Invasive Reed Adjustments

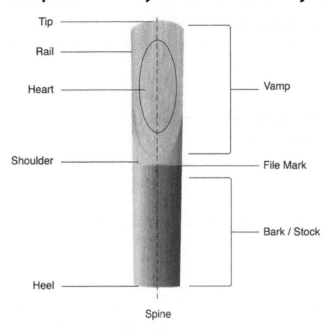

Image courtesy of D'Addario Woodwinds

There are several ways to adjust and improve the response of a reed. Some methods are very complex and "invasive" and involve a fair amount of "woodworking." For the purposes of this book, we'll focus on three simple fixes:

1. Change the placement of the reed on the mouthpiece:
   - If the reed feels a bit harder than you would like, move the reed slightly downward (away from the tip of the mouthpiece)—less than 1/16 of an inch.
   - If the reed feels a bit softer than you would like, move the reed slightly upward (toward the tip of the mouthpiece, but not beyond the tip)—less than 1/16 of an inch.
2. Seal the reed:
   - If the reel feels harder and less "free" than you would like, compress and seal the fibers by pressing the pad of your thumb hard against the reed and sliding it down the vamp toward the tip. Do this two or three times. This can be done while the reed is on the mouthpiece, or on a flat surface.
3. Adjust the reed with sandpaper:
   - To improve the seal between the reed and the mouthpiece, sand the back of the reed to make it perfectly flat. Place a piece of 600 grit wet/dry sandpaper on a flat surface, such as a piece of plexiglass. Pressing gently on the reed, move it in a figure-eight pattern on the sandpaper several times.
   - To ensure that the reed is vibrating evenly on both sides, confirm that the heart of the reed is symmetrical and tapers down toward the tip of the reed. When holding the heel of the reed and holding the reed up to a bright light, you should be able to see a darker area in the shape of an inverted "U." This darker area is the heart of the reed. If the darkness spreads more to one side than the other, lay the reed on a flat surface and very gently sand that darker area with a small piece of 600 grit wet/dry sandpaper.

Reed FAQs

What does the number on the back of the reed mean?

The number on the back of the reed denotes "strength" and increases as the reed gets harder and thicker. Reed numbers are often mistakenly referred to as "sizes." If you compare a strength 2.0 reed and a strength 3.5 reed by holding them up to the light, you'll notice that the tip of the 2.0 reed is much thinner. This allows it to vibrate more easily, lending itself as a better choice for a beginner who hasn't developed their embouchure and air support yet.

Is a harder reed strength "better"?

No! Many young players think that playing on a harder reed means that they are a better player. It is true that beginning players progress from reed strength 2.0 to 2.5 to 3, but beyond that it is personal preference and equipment pairing. Most professional classical players use strength 3 or 3.5. It is rare to find a player who uses reed strength 4.

How does a saxophonist know when they are ready to move up a reed strength?

Here are some indications:

- The sound is bright and "reedy," indicating that the reed is too soft to handle the amount of air pressure the player is using.
- The student may have trouble playing in the upper register because the reed is too thin and weak to support the sound.
- The student may be biting when they play because the reed does not offer enough resistance.

Have the student try a harder reed and see if the sound improves. High school students who play on a classical setup should usually use at least a strength 3 reed, possibly a strength 3.5. These decisions should always be made in consultation with the teacher.

How can you tell if a reed is too hard?

Here are some indications:

- A reed that is too hard will have too much resistance and sound stuffy or fuzzy.
- The player will struggle to push air through the reed and will often feel uncomfortable.

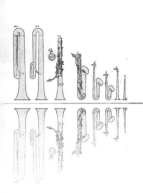

As mentioned in the introduction, the saxophone is often thought of as an instrument that is easy to play (although the truth is that it is easy to play *badly*!). As such, saxophonists sometimes place an unbalanced emphasis on technique, which can come at the expense of the music. Of course, clean and fast technique is an absolute necessity, but as teachers, it's also important to stress the importance of musicality. Like any instrument, the saxophone is simply a machine. An effective musician will be able to transcend the mechanics of that machine to create music.

There is an inextricable connection between intonation, tone, and musicality—the first fuels the second, and they then invite the third. The instrument's tone cannot be fully resonant until it's in tune, and once it is fully resonant, it will invite musical expression from a player who has cultivated that sensitivity. Because voicing is the key to those first two facets of playing the saxophone, it is essential in developing musicality as a saxophonist.

Aside from the fundamental practice of voicing to develop intonation and tone, musicality is best learned in the same way that we all learned our native spoken language—by listening. If a picture is worth a thousand words, a recording is as well. We can (and should) teach the definition of rubato and talk about the importance of phrasing and the spaces between the notes, but words can't match the results of listening to an expressive musician play something that moves you (which may be something different for each of us). Notice the use of the word "musician" rather than "saxophonist." You don't need to listen to saxophonists to learn musicality. Find recordings from the greatest artists, the artists you find most compelling, whether they play violin or cello or tuba or are singers. Then figure out what it is about their playing or singing that moves you.

Here are a few exercises to help you begin your exploration.

Exercises for Cultivating Musical Sensitivity

Focused Listening

Include at least twenty to thirty minutes of focused listening in your daily routine—perhaps as a pre-warmup. Here are some suggestions to get you started, especially geared toward the development of musical sensitivity:

Playing & Teaching the Saxophone. Allison D. Adams and Brian R. Horner, Oxford University Press. © Oxford University Press 2023.
DOI: 10.1093/oso/9780197627594.003.0035

Mischa Maisky, Schubert's "Ave Maria" from *Meditation* (Deutsche Grammaphon)

Jacqueline du Pre, Bruch's "Kol Nidrei" from *The Very Best of Jacqueline Du Pre* (EMI Classics)

Sarah Chang, Mendelssohn's "On The Wings Of Song" Op. 34 No. 2 from *Simply Sarah* (EMI Classics)

Classical Transcription

Taking the focused listening exercise one step further, choose something you've been listening to that you find especially expressive and moving. Now, learn it by ear without writing it down. Play it on your instrument, imitating every expressive nuance. Copy the vibrato, the rubato, the tone. Spend some time on this every day. Not only will it help you develop musicality, it's like superfood for your ear training. Record yourself and compare your performance to the one you are imitating. How much of what you're trying to communicate is coming through?

If you need a place to start, try transcribing the simple and beautiful melody of "Ave Maria" from the suggested Mischa Maisky recording. After that, find something that moves *you*.

"Massaging the Music"

Pick a simple, lyrical melody that you like—classical, rock, anything. Then play it by ear (no sheet music) starting on C. Listen to yourself intensely and make sure you're achieving full resonance on each note. Work your way around the circle of fourths, playing the melody in every key. Try to "massage" the music and the phrasing. Don't be afraid to overdo it—err on the side of being "too expressive." Record yourself and evaluate what you hear. Too much? Not enough?

A couple of ideas to get you started:

The Beatles' "Yesterday"

Brahms' "Lullaby"

Developing a Range of Musical Dynamics

Listening to professional musicians and developing a strong aural sense of what you are trying to communicate is an important step in the process of using dynamics. If you have a mental soundtrack of what you want to sound like and how you want to shape the musical lines, it will often happen naturally. But *how* does one create different dynamics on the saxophone? The simplest answer is that it is done by varying the volume of air being used. This can be a confusing subject because the player must *always* support the sound with strong abdominal support, whether playing soft or loud. As a general rule, a soft dynamic is created by envisioning a smaller, more narrow air stream, while a loud dynamic is created by envisioning a larger air stream. The "size" of the air stream is controlled through intensity of abdominal support because the aperture of the embouchure is not variable.

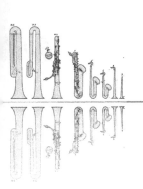

In the saxophone world in general, and at collegiate music schools in particular, there tend to be two "camps": the classical players and the jazz players. But the real world of teaching and playing requires a broad stylistic competence and the ability to be conversant in both.

It's important to note that the terms "classical" and "jazz" are used generically in this context. For example, the "classical" approach to saxophone playing is used in contemporary music and wind ensemble settings, neither of which are truly classical. In the same way, "jazz" is used in this context to refer to almost anything not "classical," such as funk, pop, world, or Americana.

A Brief History of the Saxophone in Jazz

The saxophone was invented in 1838 and used mainly in military bands until the early 1900s. It started to appear in early jazz bands in the teens and was brought squarely into the public's consciousness as a solo instrument by vaudeville-era virtuoso entertainer Rudy Wiedoeft, who made many hit recordings and helped launch a saxophone craze in the 1920s.

The instrument's presence in American popular music continued into the big band era, with the saxophone section highly visible and audible across the front row of the bands. That presence only became larger as saxophonists took center stage fronting the smaller jazz combos that emerged in the bebop era following World War II. Charlie Parker and John Coltrane were household names, and the saxophone became the instrument perhaps most associated with the genre.

Stylistic Approach

As a basic primer on the stylistic approach to jazz, we'll focus on tone, articulation, and rhythm, but as with any discussion of music, words can only go so far. Focused listening is absolutely necessary, and we've included a list of suggestions later in this chapter. Jazz, like other types of music, is a distinct dialect of the music language, and developing the ability to "speak it" fluently requires immersion.

Tone

The subject of tone has become a bit oversimplified, with the characterization of the ideal jazz tone as being "bright" and the ideal classical tone as being "dark." Certain models of

Playing & Teaching the Saxophone. Allison D. Adams and Brian R. Horner, Oxford University Press. © Oxford University Press 2023.
DOI: 10.1093/oso/9780197627594.003.0036

saxophones are said to be better for jazz because "they're brighter" or better for classical playing because "they're darker." In reality, there are artists whose tone colors fall all across the bright/dark spectrum in both genres.

Because there are fewer saxophones in a jazz big band than in a classical wind ensemble, and because a jazz combo sometimes pits the saxophone against louder instruments, such as drums or electric guitar, the player must produce a tone that can be heard in these settings. The tone is sometimes referred to as having "edge" or being able to "cut through." This need to be heard is one of the reasons that players typically use a different mouthpiece in a jazz setting than they do in a classical setting. There are a number of jazz mouthpieces on the market, and they have physical characteristics that aid in this mission—larger tip openings, longer facings, and larger chambers, when compared to classical mouthpieces. Although subject to personal preference, these mouthpieces should be paired with "jazz reeds," offered by all the mainstream reed manufacturers. These reeds are typically cut to be slightly thinner so that they vibrate more freely and offer less resistance and back pressure.

As with classical mouthpieces, there are many (probably more!) brands and models of jazz mouthpieces available—in metal, hard rubber, even wood! The selection process will be led by your tonal concept and listening tastes. Although your own physical characteristics and voicing manipulations have a huge impact on the sound you produce, a mouthpiece used to produce a tone like Stan Getz's has different physical attributes than a mouthpiece used to produce a tone like Michael Brecker's. Mouthpiece selection should be made in consultation with a saxophone jazz specialist whenever possible.

In addition to added "loudness," a jazz setup (the combination of mouthpiece and reed) also allows the player more *flexibility* of tone, another hallmark of the style. Pitch bends and various tonal inflections are common expressive elements in jazz, and although voicing plays a huge role, appropriate equipment will allow an even greater palette.

Rhythm

The most obvious difference in the approach to rhythm in the context of jazz is the practice of "swinging" the eighth notes. Although they're written the same as "straight" eighth notes, swing eighths are weighted unequally so that the first one in a pair is longer in duration than the second. As with tone, listening is the fastest and best path to understanding this rhythmic concept. There's a widely held misconception that a transcription of the literal rhythm of swing eighth notes would look like this:

A transcription that gets much closer to the sound and laid-back feel of swing eighths is this:

Played with swing eighths, these two G scales will sound the same:

This understanding of the rhythm allows the melodic lines to stay smooth as the tempo increases, resulting in eighth note lines that sound almost straight at the blistering tempos of, say, a Charlie Parker solo.

It should be noted that there are some types of jazz where swing eighths are not appropriate, such as funk music or ballads. In jazz ensemble sheet music, there is often a notation to help the players ("straight eighths" etc.) but seeking out a professional recording of the tune will likely answer any questions regarding proper performance practice.

Articulation

As with swing eighth notes, there's a manner of articulating eighth note lines that is understood as a matter of performance practice, well-established and understood within the tradition. In eighth note lines, the upbeats should be articulated and accented slightly, giving the music the feeling of moving forward. Even when no slurs are written (and they likely won't be), only the upbeats are tongued.

Agreement across the saxophone section of a jazz ensemble on matters such as articulation, accents, and rhythm are obviously just as important as in any other type of large or small ensemble. These details, executed in the same way together, will elevate the impact of that section.

Introduction to Improvisation

We're all improvising all the time. When we speak, we constantly put words together to form sentences, group sentences together to form coherent trains of thought, and engage in a cycle of listening to others and responding to create conversations. In music, notes are our words, phrases are our ideas, and interactions with the other musicians are our conversations. But there's probably nothing scarier for students in the band room than the notion of improvising in front of their peers. Here are a few tools and an exercise to help change that.

1. Start Simple

   You don't need to play a lot of notes to play an effective solo. Start with one note and play around with the rhythm. Then add one more note. Repeat.

2. Use Silence

   You don't need to fill all the space. If you finish an idea, take some space to listen and come up with the next idea, one that will be informed by what you heard.

3. "Mess with" the Song's Melody and Rhythm

   If you're improvising over a song that has a melody (as opposed to playing over something that might just be a groove), use that melody as your starting point. Let's use "Mary Had a Little Lamb" as an example. Pretend you've just played the melody. For your solo, you might try something like this:

4. Create Short Melodies

   When we speak, we don't fire out a hundred rapid-fire words that have no apparent organization. We speak in thoughts, in phrases. Mimic this in your musical improvising. Focus on creating a melody that is hummable. Make up a melody in your head—it can be any length. Sing or hum it. Play it. Eventually, you'll be able to string these thoughts together.

5. Practice Playing By Ear in All Twelve Keys

Take any melody you can think of (preferably something that's familiar, like "Happy Birthday") and play it by ear starting on any note. Then, pick out the melody in all twelve keys, working your way around the circle of fourths. This develops your ability to hear something in your head and play it on your instrument—the ultimate goal of the improvising musician.

There are a number of play-along products available that provide audio and chord changes, allowing endless practice and experimentation. The most famous have been released by jazz pedagogue Jamey Aebersold over the last fifty years, now available digitally.

Let's Explore!

The "No Sheet Music Blues" is, fittingly, just a background—there's no sheet music for the melody. That's up to you. Find a friend and take turns improvising using some of the tools and strategies we've discussed while the other plays the background figures. If you want to work on it alone, record the background on your phone.

Don't overthink it at this point and experiment using notes in the concert B♭ scale. If you don't like how one sounds, use a different one!

No Sheet Music Blues

Alto or Baritone Saxophone

Soprano or Tenor Saxophone

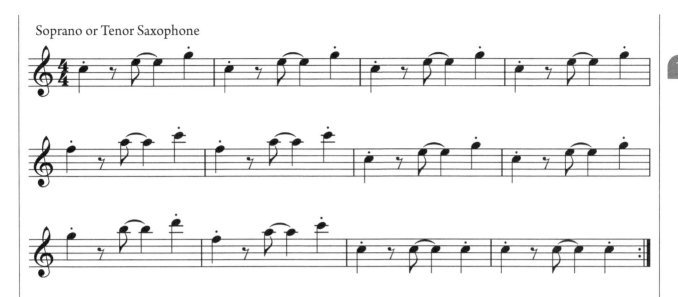

Let's take it a step further. We're still going to work with the same twelve-bar blues accompaniment, but this time we'll think of it as the "Cheat Sheet Blues." As before, take turns playing the background and improvising over it. Stick with the same concepts you were just exploring (stay simple, use silence, create short melodies), but this time use the notes in the blues scale, taking turns with your partner. The blues scale comprises scale degrees 1, ♭3, 4, ♭5, 5, and ♭7:

Listen to yourself. Which notes do you like with which chords? Trust your ears.

Now, do the same thing again, but use the notes in the pentatonic scale. The pentatonic scale is made up of scale degrees 1, 2, 3, 5, and 6:

Talking the Talk: Terms You Might Hear in Jazz Band

"Back to the head!"

Generally speaking, the performance of a jazz tune includes playing the melody, then repeating the chord progression to accompany improvised solos, then playing the melody again. In jazz parlance, the melody is called "the head" and at the close of the solo section the bandleader might give the band a cue—"back to the head!"

"Let's open it up for solos"

When discussing the "roadmap" for a piece, you might hear the band director say that a certain section will be "open." That just means that the section will be repeated while various players take improvised solos over the section's chord progression.

"It's just a blues . . . "

As mentioned above, the performance of a jazz tune generally includes improvised solos over the chord progression. Chord progressions vary in complexity and a blues progression (usually a "twelve-bar blues") is one of the simplest and most common progressions. An example of a simple form of a twelve-bar blues in B♭ (as seen above in the "No Sheet Music Blues") would be four measures of the I chord (the tonic, which is B♭ in this case), two measures of the IV chord (a chord built on the 4th scale degree, E♭ in this case), two measures of the I chord, one measure of the V chord (F in this case), one measure of the IV chord (E♭ again), ending with two measures of the I chord. A player stepping onto the stage at a jam session might be relieved to hear "it's just a blues in B♭."

"Practice your ii-V-I patterns in all keys" (verbalized as "2, 5, 1")

Jazz chord progressions can range from being fairly simple, staying on a single chord for multiple measures, to being much more complex, with chords changing with each beat. Part of the process of developing a jazz vocabulary is to learn certain patterns in all keys that you can retrieve from your aural and muscle memory while you're improvising. A common "turnaround" in chord progressions is the "ii-V7-I," a chord built on the second scale degree (a minor chord, since it is built using notes that are diatonic to the first scale degree), a chord built on the fifth scale degree (it's a dominant chord because of the notes available in the tonic key, and because it leads somewhere), and an arrival on a chord built on the tonic, or the I.

Here is an example of a pattern that follows this progression:

Alto/Bari Saxophone:

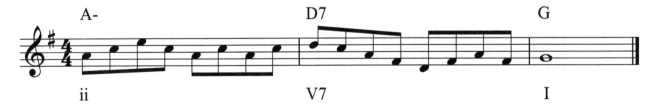

Tenor/Soprano Saxophone:

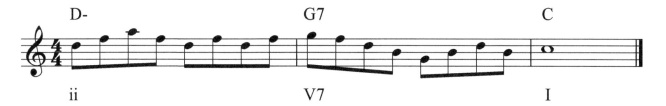

If you play a solo over a ii-V7-I turnaround that doesn't highlight those chords, the band director may urge you to "practice your ii-V-I patterns in all keys."

"Trade 4's"

Let's say your band is in the middle of the solo section of a twelve-bar-blues and the band director shouts, "trade 4's!" She's helping the band to increase the excitement of the solo section by asking the players to change soloists every four bars, rather than once every twelve-bar chorus. A musical duel usually ensues and it's exciting for everyone, audience and players alike. Sometimes traded sections will start with trading eights, then fours, then twos, with the excitement building as the traded solos get shorter. This is often agreed upon loosely beforehand, or it may just develop in the moment.

"We'll vamp at the end"

As you can see from the items we've discussed, a tune performed in jazz band can have more of a "choose-your-own-adventure" feel than a typical classical or band piece, with structural decisions made by the performers. Another common decision (and sometimes it's an instruction in the music) is to vamp a section, repeating it on a loop until the signal is given to move on. The end of a tune is a common place for this to happen.

Quick Start Guide to Jazz Listening

When approaching the monumental task of listening to jazz in an effort to familiarize yourself with the genre, it makes sense to start with a chronological approach. Starting at the beginning, with Louis Armstrong, allows you to develop a sense of the stylistic arc of the genre as a whole.

Below is a group of suggestions to start you on your way. Each of these artists is iconic in their own right, so if any of these albums grab you, there's more where they came from. Check out the artist on Wikipedia, read about the album, the personnel, what came before and after—go down the rabbit hole and enjoy! This is by no means an exhaustive or comprehensive list—we could list recommended artists and albums for many pages!

Louis Armstrong, *The Best of the Hot 5 & Hot 7 Recordings* (Recordings from 1926–1928, Sony Legacy)

Duke Ellington, *Never No Lament: The Blanton-Webster Band* (Recordings from 1940–1942, Bluebird)

Charlie Parker, *The Complete Savoy & Dial Master Takes* (Recordings from 1945–1948, Savoy)

Stan Getz, *Stan Getz Plays* (1955, Verve)

Miles Davis, *Kind of Blue* (1959, Columbia)

Cannonball Adderley, *Them Dirty Blues* (1960, Riverside)

John Coltrane, *Ascension* (1966, Impulse!)

Miles Davis, *Bitches Brew* (1970, Columbia)

Michael Brecker, *The Very Best of Michael Brecker* (Recordings from 1987–2006, Verve)

James Carter, *In Carterian Fashion* (1998, Atlantic)

Joshua Redman Elastic Band, *Momentum* (2005, Nonesuch)

Kamasi Washington, *The Epic* (2015, Brainfeeder)

SOPRANO, TENOR, AND BARITONE SAXOPHONE

37

Although saxophonists often start on alto saxophone (and sometimes tenor), they will need to have the skills to play other instruments in the saxophone family to fill a concert band or jazz band section. These tips will help students adapt to playing various members of the saxophone family.

For specific brands of instruments, mouthpieces, reeds, etc., see Chapter 44, "Saxophone Equipment."

When students are switching to another member of the saxophone family, they should:

1. Check for the proper amount of mouthpiece with the Index Card Trick (see Chapter 6, "Embouchure").
2. Check for the proper mouthpiece pitch on mouthpiece/reed only (see Chapter 33, "Intonation Training.")
3. Practice overtones to adjust voicing to the new instrument (see Chapter 30, "Voicing and Overtones: The First Overtone" and Chapter 31, "Voicing and Overtones: The Second Overtone").

Soprano Saxophone

Posture

The soprano should not be held vertically like a clarinet—it must be held out away from the body with the head turned down slightly so that the mouthpiece enters the mouth at the same angle as the other saxophones.

Playing Considerations

- Soprano saxophone is more difficult to control than the other saxophones in terms of tone, intonation, and voicing.
  - A new soprano player should spend a lot of time with drones and the tuner.
- Tongue position is generally higher than alto (the "hee" position is a bit more exaggerated).
- A lot of air support is needed, but be careful not to overblow.
- If a student plays the soprano with alto voicing/air, the tone is spread and the tuning is not correct.
  - Encourage students to explore the second overtone exercises to help find correct air/voicing (Chapter 31, "Voicing and Overtones: The Second Overtone").

Playing & Teaching the Saxophone. Allison D. Adams and Brian R. Horner, Oxford University Press. © Oxford University Press 2023.
DOI: 10.1093/oso/9780197627594.003.0037

Additional Considerations

- Put your best alto saxophone player on soprano if possible!
- A low-quality soprano saxophone will often have extensive tuning issues.

Tenor Saxophone

Posture

The tenor saxophone should always be held to the side of the body when sitting. Be sure the instrument's neck is turned enough to allow the student to hold it to the side, but not so far that it causes the octave vent to leak.

Playing Considerations

- Bigger horn = lots of air needed.
- D (fourth line of the staff) and G (above the staff) can be finicky notes. This is normal, and the player will need to become familiar with the specific voicing required for each.
- Reeds are larger and can dry out and warp (get wavy on the end). This can be avoided through proper storage and rotation of reeds.

Additional Considerations

The octave vent mechanism on the tenor sax neck is very delicate. It is easy for students to put too much pressure on it when putting the neck onto the body. If the mechanism is bent, the vent on top of the neck will not seal and can make it very difficult to play the instrument. This will be apparent when the student plays in the middle register and the notes crack/squawk. See the chapter on saxophone maintenance (Chapter 45) for information on how to fix this.

Baritone Saxophone

Posture

The baritone saxophone should always be held to the side of the body. Adjust the neck strap and saxophone neck position so the student can sit straight up. It is a heavy instrument, so students may want to purchase a harness to help distribute weight to the shoulders.

- Neotech is a brand that makes good student-level harnesses.
- Make sure the harness is adjusted correctly.

Playing Considerations

- Bigger horn = lots of air needed.
- Middle D is a finicky note that sometimes cracks. This is normal, and the player will need to become familiar with its specific voicing.

- In general, voicing for baritone involves a more open oral cavity, but the tongue must still be in the "hee" position for most notes and especially upper register notes.
- Sloppy articulation is very common because the reed is large:
  - Make sure students use a "DOO" (rather than "TAH") articulation.
  - Tongue touches back molars and moves back away from reed.
- The mouthpiece is bigger, but students must make sure their embouchure is not too loose. All embouchure concepts for alto saxophone apply!
- Reeds are larger and can dry out and warp (get wavy on the end). This can be avoided through proper storage and rotation of reeds.

Additional Considerations

- Due to the high cost of replacing a baritone saxophone, many school-owned instruments are very old and in considerable disrepair.
- Make sure a young student has big enough hands for the instrument.
- Be sure the instrument is in good condition. Due to their size and weight, baritone saxophones tend to get knocked around and can fall out of adjustment easily.
- Some marching bands include baritone saxophone, but it's physically very demanding and not recommended.

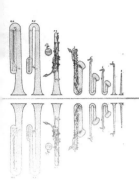

The altissimo register of the saxophone refers to the pitches above palm F♯ (above the staff). These notes are not usually found in the saxophone parts of standard band literature, but they are used by college-level and professional saxophonists in solo and chamber repertoire. Many high school saxophonists begin to explore the altissimo register, and it is fun and satisfying to master the notes of the upper register.

Overtones: The Key to the Altissimo Register

The foundation of this method book is based upon the development of voicing and overtones for young players. Voicing and overtones are crucial for good tone and tuning, but this flexibility is also the key to playing in the upper register of the saxophone.

Altissimo pitches are essentially overtones of specific finger combinations. To play altissimo notes, a saxophonist must know the correct fingering to use, but must also have the flexibility of voicing needed for that fingering to produce the correct overtone, or altissimo pitch.

If you are interested in developing your altissimo register, focus on mastering the overtone and voicing exercises found in this book.

Playing & Teaching the Saxophone. Allison D. Adams and Brian R. Horner, Oxford University Press. © Oxford University Press 2023.
DOI: 10.1093/oso/9780197627594.003.0038

Front Fingerings: The Bridge to the Altissimo Register

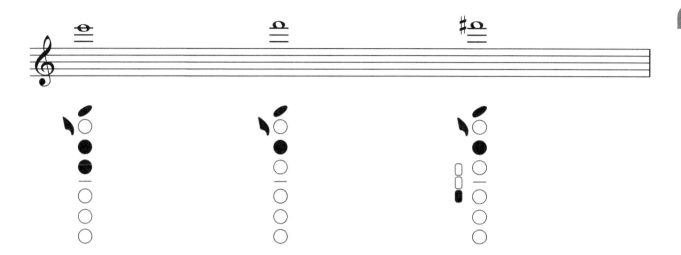

You have already learned the palm key fingerings for the notes listed above. The fingerings listed here are called "front fingerings." They are useful fingerings for many passages, but they are also fingerings that bridge the upper register of the saxophone to the altissimo register.

Exercise 1

Here is a good exercise to start with:

Exercise 2

Front F and E are relatively easy to produce. Front F♯ is usually more difficult and will require patience, voicing exploration, and repetition to master.

Altissimo Fingerings

For each note in the altissimo register, remember that the fingering must be paired with its correct voicing. The study of overtones has prepared you to find this through exploration of exaggerated tongue positions and the resulting throat shapes. This must be practiced with patience and repetition!

Here are some of the most common fingerings for the first altissimo notes:

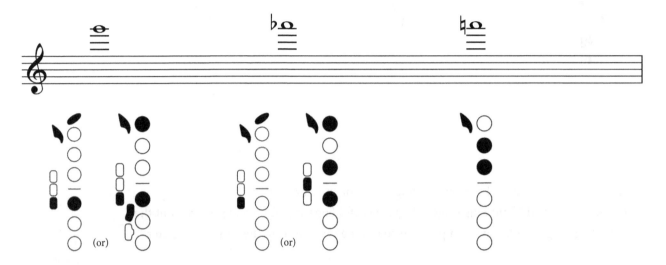

Visit Chapter 48, "Saxophone Resource Guide," for further reading on the altissimo range.

The saxophone is a very versatile instrument that can produce a lot of sounds outside of the usual pitches associated with traditional Western music. These sounds are called "extended techniques."

Below is a brief description of various extended techniques and an example of how they are often notated. Most of these will not appear in traditional band music or high school solo literature, but they are important to be aware of as they are becoming more and more common in new literature.

1. *Growling*: Singing while playing.
   - Notated with "growl" written over the pitch and slashes through the stem.

2. *Flutter Tongue*: Creating a disturbance of the air while playing, creating a sound that purrs or flutters.
   - There are two techniques:
     1. Roll the front of the tongue, much like the production of a Spanish "r" while the back of the tongue stays in the "hee" position, anchored to the insides of the upper back molars.
     2. Roll the back of the throat to produce the same effect, much like the sensation of gurgling water. The uvula (the part that hangs down into the throat from the roof of the mouth) vibrates to produce this effect.
   - Notated with "flatt." or "flutter" written over the note and slashes through the stem.

3. *Multiphonics*: Using a fingering that sounds multiple pitches.
   - Often requires a certain placement of the embouchure on the reed to speak correctly (more or less mouthpiece than what is usually used).

Playing & Teaching the Saxophone. Allison D. Adams and Brian R. Horner, Oxford University Press. © Oxford University Press 2023.
DOI: 10.1093/oso/9780197627594.003.0039

- Affected by mouthpiece, reed, and make/model of horn. Some fingerings do not speak as easily on certain setups.
- If this is used in a piece of music, the composer will often include the fingering for the performer along with a notation for the pitches that should result.

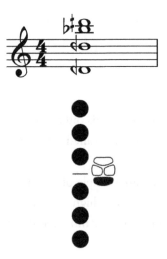

4. *Slap Tongue*: Creating a percussive sound by suctioning the tongue to the reed and closing off the reed, then pulling the tongue down quickly. There are two standard types of slap tonguing: open slaps and closed slaps. Slap notation is sometimes variable, but the composer will often write "slap" over it to be clear.
    - "*Closed slap*": a slightly pitched percussive sound. The amount of pitch can be varied. Successive closed slap-tonguing is difficult to do at quick tempos. The embouchure stays sealed to produce this effect.
    - "*Open slap*": a loud, unpitched, percussive sound caused by creating a seal on the reed with the tongue, then lowering the entire jaw and opening the mouth.

5. *Circular Breathing*: Playing continuously while storing air in the cheeks and using the cheek muscles to push the air out, allowing time to quickly breathe in through the nose without interrupting the sound. This is difficult in extreme registers, due to the large mass of air required to play low and the intensity of air pressure required to play high.
    - Usually not a notated technique—the player will choose where they use this.

6. *Key Clicks*: Creating a percussive sound with the keys.
    - Note: The sound produced from this technique is very quiet. While it can come across well in a solo section, within an ensemble context, it is difficult to hear if the saxophonist is not amplified.

7. *Quarter Tones*: Using a fingering to create intervals smaller than a half step.

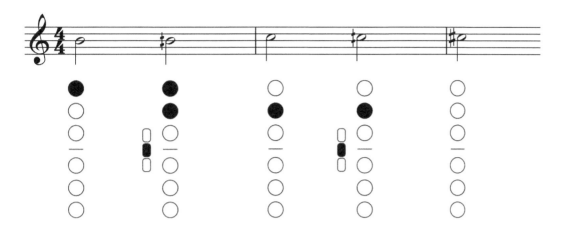

8. *Timbre Trills (Bisbigliando)*: Using fingerings to create changes in timbre by opening and closing the appropriate key—pitch varies only slightly (as opposed to a trill between two different notes).
   - Usually soft, subtle, and rapid.
   - Notated with "bisbi." written over the pitch.

9. *Irregular Vibrato*: A piece of contemporary music may include specific instructions regarding vibrato, such as showing a picture over the note to indicate an irregular or extra wide use of vibrato. In this case, the player should do their best to make the aural speed and depth of the vibrato match the visual depiction. Irregular vibrato is often shown with this type of notation above a sustained pitch:

10. *Subtone*: Very, very quiet dynamic, easiest to produce in low registers. Often has an airy quality in the low register.
    - Notated with "subtone" written over the pitches:

11. *Teeth on Reed*: Will produce a high shrieking or squealing sound on undefined pitches.
    - Notation can vary, but it is often indicated with a triangular note head several ledger lines above the staff, often accompanied with the text *"teeth on reed."*

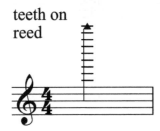

Visit Chapter 48, "Saxophone Resource Guide," for further reading on extended techniques.

PART 4 Teaching Tools

"First Lesson Planning Guide" (Chapter 41) is a step-by-step guide to help you easily navigate the details of assembly, embouchure, first sounds, and disassembly for beginning students.

"Troubleshooting" (Chapter 42) provides a list of the most common problems you'll encounter among your students and the most likely fixes.

"Saxophone Pitch Tendency Guide" (Chapter 43) is a quick-reference guide to the intonation problems that are inherent to the instrument, with suggested countermeasures.

"Saxophone Equipment" (Chapter 44) provides information to help you advise your students as they navigate the many brands of saxophones, mouthpieces, reeds, ligatures, and other gear.

"Saxophone Maintenance" (Chapter 45) discusses how to keep saxophones playable in the short and long term, including simple band room fixes for common issues.

"Wellness for the Young Musician" (Chapter 46) provides a guide to establishing good habits, including a simple stretching routine, strategies to decrease performance anxiety, and a summary of common wellness practices.

"Suggested Practice Routine and Warm-Ups" (Chapter 47) outlines a routine to guide students toward becoming their own best teacher.

Concluding this section, Chapter 48 ("Saxophone Resource Guide") provides suggestions for listening, repertoire, and further reading.

Playing & Teaching the Saxophone. Allison D. Adams and Brian R. Horner, Oxford University Press. © Oxford University Press 2023.
DOI: 10.1093/oso/9780197627594.003.0040

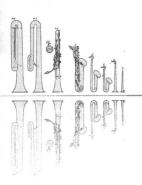

Below is a sample of what the first saxophone lesson might look like. This is not the only way it can be done, but is meant to provide an example of clear, specific directions that may be helpful as you find your own style. Be sure to model for your students as much as possible!

Objectives

1. Students will demonstrate proper care of the saxophone.
2. Students will be able to put the saxophone together correctly.
3. Students will successfully produce their first sounds on the neck/mouthpiece and the notes B, A, and G on the instrument.
4. Students will be able to take the saxophone apart correctly.

The Lesson

Caring For the Saxophone

1. Set the case on the floor to the right of their chair, or on a stable surface, such a nearby table.
   - Make sure each student knows how to tell that their particular case is right-side-up. There is often a company logo on the top side of the case.
2. Allow students to open the case. If the case is on the floor, have the student kneel on the floor as well.
   - "Wow, look how beautiful your instrument is! It's so shiny!"
3. Establish rules.
   - The students must understand that instruments are expensive and fragile, and that it is very important that they are taken care of properly so that they don't break.
   - The students, teacher, and parents are the only people allowed to touch the instrument—not their friends or siblings (unless adult permission is given).
   - The students should brush their teeth, drink water, and wash their hands before taking the instrument out of the case.
4. Check the contents of the case.
   - Introduce each part of the instrument (neck strap, mouthpiece, ligature, reeds, neck, body, swab).
   - Teach the students how to take each piece out, name it, hold it, and put it back.

Playing & Teaching the Saxophone. Allison D. Adams and Brian R. Horner, Oxford University Press. © Oxford University Press 2023.
DOI: 10.1093/oso/9780197627594.003.0041

Assembly Instructions

1. Put on the neck strap and cinch up the clasp to the bottom of the collarbone so it will be easy to adjust downward later.
   - "This is always the first thing we do when we put the saxophone together and it's very important!"
2. Take out a reed very carefully and soak the thin end in your mouth or in a cup of water
   - Must always have two to three good reeds at a time (four would be best). For now, a "good reed" is one that is clean and is not broken.
     - Never touch the thin tip of the reed. If the tip of the reed breaks, the reed won't work properly.
3. Take out the saxophone neck. Be careful not to apply pressure to the octave vent mechanism.
   - Apply cork grease to the cork on the end of the neck.
     - "Do this every time you practice this week!"
4. Turn the reed around and soak the thick end in your mouth or in a cup of water.
5. Put the mouthpiece on the neck using gentle twists.
6. Carefully put the reed on the mouthpiece.
   - Hold the reed by the sides (never touching the thin tip).
   - The smooth, flat part of the reed will fit against the flat part on the mouthpiece.
   - Move the ligature up so that there's enough space for the reed to slide under. Then slide the thick part of the reed down from the tip of the mouthpiece and under the ligature.
   - The tip of the reed should line up with the tip of the mouthpiece.
   - Be careful to never touch the tip of the reed, as it is very fragile.
   - The ligature should be placed over the bark of the reed. Tighten the ligature screws (there may be one or two) just enough to hold the reed securely on the mouthpiece and keep the ligature in place. Be careful not to overtighten or the screws might break.

If you are sitting or kneeling on the floor with your students to put the instrument together, be sure to move to chairs now.

The First Sounds and Articulation—On Neck and Mouthpiece Only

1. Hold the neck/mouthpiece gently in a fist just below the mouthpiece, being careful not to apply pressure to the octave vent mechanism.
2. Embouchure (model each step for the students).
   - Define term "embouchure," discussing the muscles of the lips and mouth in the context of how they hold the saxophone mouthpiece.
   - Demonstrate how to determine how much mouthpiece to use.
     - Using an index card and pencil, find the spot where the reed and mouthpiece meet. Draw a line on the reed.
   - Describe the steps to forming a correct embouchure.

1. Rest your top teeth on top of mouthpiece, directly above the line you drew on the reed.
2. Tuck about half of your bottom lip over your bottom teeth.
3. Close your lips around the mouthpiece as if forming a circle.

Remind students that the chin should be flat and relaxed—never bunched—and that the tongue should be in the "hee" position.

3. Breathing
   - Drop the jaw and relax the corners of the mouth to breathe.
   - Keep the top teeth resting on top of mouthpiece.
4. Posture
   - Sit up straight with feet flat on the floor.
   - Bring the mouthpiece toward the mouth.
   - The mouthpiece should go straight into the mouth, with the top of the neck (with the octave mechanism) parallel to the floor.
5. Review embouchure/breathing/posture steps, first without making any sound and then adding sound.
6. Check that students are able to match Concert G♯ (alto/bari) and are not puffing their cheeks.
7. Articulation
   - After starting the sound with air, be sure students can start the sound using their tongue on the reed.
   - Use the method outlined in Chapter 9, "AIR-ticulation."

The First Sounds—With the Entire Instrument

1. Teach students the proper way to pick up the saxophone body and attach it to the neck strap.
   - If cases are on the floor, have students kneel on the floor next to the case to get the body out.
2. Playing position.
   - Hold the saxophone between the legs (without resting instrument on the chair) or to the right side, depending on the height of the student.
   - Check that the neck strap is high enough that the mouthpiece comes directly to the mouth while the student sits up straight. It is important that the student does not raise their head to meet the mouthpiece.
3. Hand position (model for students).
   - LH on top:
     - Fingers on pearls.
     - Thumb rests on circular thumb pad.
   - RH on bottom:
     - Fingers on pearls.
     - Thumb rests under thumb hook on the back.

- Pinkies relax in front of, not behind, the pinky keys.
- Fingers should be naturally curved and relaxed.

4. Teach B, A, G using tongued articulation.
- Teach fingering for B.
- Model playing a B.
- Students play a B.
- Repeat with A, then G.

5. With those notes, students can go home and try out some simple songs, such as *Mary Had a Little Lamb*, *Hot Cross Buns*, etc. (see assignment at end of chapter).

Disassembly

1. If the saxophone case is on the floor, be sure to kneel next to the case.
2. Unscrew the neck screw, take off the neck/mouthpiece, and place it *in a safe place*.
3. Swab the body.
   - Place the weight of the swab in the saxophone bell, letting it rest in the crook of the instrument.
   - Gently turn the saxophone upside down so that the weight drops out the smaller end of the saxophone tube.
   - Carefully pull the string until the swab comes out the smaller end of the saxophone.
   - Near the top of the instrument there is a small rod that protrudes into the body of the saxophone. Be very careful that the swab does not get stuck on this rod.
4. Place the plug in the hole at the top of the saxophone body.
5. Put the saxophone body in case.
   - Hold the saxophone by the bell with one hand, and the top of body with other hand.
   - Do not hold the saxophone by the keys/rods.
6. Carefully take the reed off the mouthpiece.
   - Unscrew the ligature and push it up slightly on the mouthpiece to release the reed.
   - Push up on the bottom of the reed, or hold the reed by the sides, to bring it up and off of the mouthpiece.
   - Place the reed in its case, being very careful not to break the tip.
     - If using a plastic case with an opening on the side, put the thick part of the reed in before the tip.
   - Place the reed case into the saxophone case.
7. Take the neck and mouthpiece apart using gentle twists. Be careful not to put pressure on the octave key mechanism. Place the neck in the saxophone case.
8. Put the mouthpiece cap on and place the mouthpiece/ligature in the saxophone case.
9. Lower the neck strap clasp and take the neck strap off over the head. Place it in the saxophone case.
10. Close and latch the saxophone case. Be sure the case is latched before picking it up, or the saxophone may fall and become damaged.

First Assignment: Hand-It-Over Worksheet 🖹

1. Play Concert G♯ on the alto neck/mouthpiece.
2. Practice articulation on the neck/mouthpiece.
3. Review fingerings for B, A, G.
4. Three-note songs: *Mary Had a Little Lamb, Hot Cross Buns*, etc.

Please see companion website to download the detailed assignment worksheet to distribute to students.

One of the most important skills that a music instructor must have is the ability to diagnose a problem and present an appropriate solution. This chapter lists many of the common problems seen among younger students, along with suggestions on how to address the issue.

Issues Related to Response

Struggling to Make a Sound

Check the reed

1. Is it chipped?
2. Is it lined up perfectly on the mouthpiece?
3. Was the reed soaked long enough? A dry reed will not vibrate properly.
4. What is the reed strength? A reed that is too hard for the player will not vibrate properly.

Check embouchure

1. Are the three basic steps of embouchure correct?
   • Rest the top teeth on top of mouthpiece.
   • Tuck about half of the bottom lip over the bottom teeth.
   • Close the lips around the mouthpiece as if forming a circle.
2. Are they using too little mouthpiece?
   • Lips should be at the spot where the reed and mouthpiece meet. Check this spot by sliding an index card carefully between the reed and mouthpiece. The spot where it stops is the same spot where the bottom lip and top teeth should be placed.
3. Are the top and bottom lips in line with one another? A chin that is pushing forward may close off the sound.
4. Is the embouchure too tight?
   • If the bottom lip is squeezing too hard, it chokes the reed and keeps it from vibrating/producing a sound. A bunched chin is a good indication that the bottom lip is applying upward pressure.

Playing & Teaching the Saxophone. Allison D. Adams and Brian R. Horner, Oxford University Press. © Oxford University Press 2023.
DOI: 10.1093/oso/9780197627594.003.0042

Low Notes Don't Speak

1. Use more air.
2. Discuss voicing. The back of the tongue shifts down for the lower notes (a feeling similar to yawning). See Chapter 15, "Voicing and Overtones for Low Notes," for more detail.
3. Make sure the student is not biting and applying upward pressure on the reed, which would restrict air flow and cause the higher octave to sound. Check that they have a good anchor with the top teeth resting on top of the mouthpiece.
4. Make sure correct posture is being used. If the mouthpiece is coming into the mouth at an angle that is too steep (more like clarinet position), it can result in too much pressure on the reed. This may cause the higher octave to sound.
5. Check for a leak in the pads at the bottom end of the instrument. Small leaks will need to be detected with a leak light, but larger ones may be visible. Close the pads by fingering the low note and look to see if they are closing completely on the tone holes.

   NOTE: Do not encourage students to lower the jaw to improve low note response!

Student is Struggling to Navigate Between Middle Register Notes (especially B, C, C♯) and Fourth-line D

1. Discuss voicing. Moving between middle C and middle D is tricky because of the dramatic change from one finger to many. Also, middle D is the first note to use the octave key; therefore, it requires a shift in voicing. When voiced incorrectly, many students will experience a crack in the sound when going between these notes. Try the voicing suggestions below:
   • Middle C: "Hee" tongue position (default playing position). These notes can be very flat if correct voicing is not used
   • Middle D: Tongue position stays high, but the throat is open like a yawn.
2. Check finger coordination. The fingers need to move exactly together, including the addition of the left thumb on the octave key when going to middle D. This should be practiced very slowly.
3. Ask them to use more air. When moving from "short-tube" notes, such as B, C, and C♯, to "long-tube" notes, such as middle D, more air is needed to compensate for the change in tube length. Many more keys are closed for middle D.

Notes Are "Chirping" an Octave Higher Even When Octave Key is Not Depressed

1. The octave vent key on the neck may be propped open.
   • Loosen the neck screw and move the neck right and left while watching the octave vent key on top of the neck. Is there a spot where it closes completely?
2. The octave key mechanism may be bent.
   • With the neck on the body, observe the contact between the body post and the neck mechanism. From this, you should be able to tell how it needs to be bent back into place.
   • Take the neck off and gently hold the key down while using pressure to bend and adjust the metal loop around the bottom of the neck.

- Put the neck back on the body and see if the adjustment aligned the parts into proper contact.

Strange Squawks

1. Make sure the student isn't pushing down extra keys--especially the right-hand side keys or left-hand palm keys--when fingering the note.
2. Confirm that all keys are moving up and down as they should--sometimes a popped spring will disrupt the intended fingering.

Issues Related to Tone

Remember that tone is greatly affected by embouchure, voicing, air, and posture. Continue to insist on correct fundamentals.

Squeaks In the Sound

When you hear squeaks in the sound, it usually means that there is an imbalance in how the reed is vibrating. This is very common among beginner students! Check the following:

1. The reed
   - Is the reed on the mouthpiece correctly?
   - Is the reed wet enough? A dry reed will not vibrate evenly.
   - Is the reed chipped or cracked?
   - How old is the reed? As reeds get older, they may dry out unevenly. If you take the reed off the mouthpiece and look at the back, you'll be able to see if one side is dry.
   - Is the reed the correct strength for the student?
2. Embouchure
   - The embouchure needs to provide consistent pressure. Go through the basic steps of embouchure formation. Is the student anchoring their top teeth on top of the mouthpiece? Are they tucking the correct amount of bottom lip? Are they bringing corners forward to form a circular embouchure around the mouthpiece?
3. Posture
   - Is the student's neck strap at the proper height so that the saxophone mouthpiece comes in at the correct angle?
   - Does the student have the neck and mouthpiece set up correctly so that their head is not tilted?
4. Air
   - Encourage your student to use more air. Playing with a small amount of air may cause a student to tighten the embouchure.
5. Equipment
   - In rare cases, a student who struggles with squeaks may need a different mouthpiece. Most stock mouthpieces are fine for beginner players, but occasionally you may find one that is cut incorrectly. If this is the case, there may not be much the student can do. Have them try a different stock mouthpiece to see if it helps!

Notes Have a "Wobbly" Sound

1. Use more air.
2. Check embouchure for proper formation.
3. Pads may be leaking.

Tone Sounds "Spitty"

It is very common for condensation or saliva to rattle around in the mouthpiece and disrupt the purity of the tone.

1. Suck in through the mouthpiece before starting to play, much like drinking a Slurpee through a straw. This will help clear out any condensation. Professional players do this constantly before starting a phrase to avoid the problem. It takes a little practice, but it can be done quietly.
2. Encourage students to swallow any extra saliva in their mouth before playing.
3. Dab a small amount of olive oil on the inside beak of the mouthpiece.

Tone is Small and Unstable, Lacks Resonance

1. There is not enough mouthpiece in mouth. If the neck strap is up too high or if the student is resting their saxophone on their chair or knee, it will cause the player to take in too little of the mouthpiece.
2. Use proper air support.
3. The reed may be too hard or too soft by approximately a full strength. If it's too hard, it is too resistant to allow air through. If it's too soft it may close off against the mouthpiece and choke the sound.
4. The reed may be too dry and unable to vibrate, or the reed may be warped (if the tip is wavy, take it off the mouthpiece and smooth it out on a flat surface by pushing your finger along the fibers).
5. The chin may be bunched.
   - If bunched, concentrate on a round embouchure rather than one that pulls the corners of the mouth back. The chin should look flat.
6. The bottom lip may be obstructing sound.
   - If the lower lip protrudes forward (looking like a pout), move it further into the mouth over the teeth.
   - If the red part of your lower lip is completely covered up, you are probably tucking in too much bottom lip. This will restrict vibration of the reed.

Tone Is Reedy or Bright

1. The reed may be too soft by approximately a half-strength.
2. The student may be playing on a mouthpiece that cultivates a bright sound, such as a jazz mouthpiece.

Tone Is Stuffy, Airy, or Unfocused

1. The reed may be too hard by approximately a half-strength.
2. Are the top teeth anchored on top of the mouthpiece? The top teeth and top lip should never come off the top of the mouthpiece while playing or breathing.
3. Are cheeks puffing out? Cheeks should never puff out–keep them pulled in against the teeth.

Tone is Wild or Out-of-Control

1. There is too much mouthpiece in mouth.
2. The air stream is not focused enough.

Issues Related to Tuning

See Chapter 33 ("Intonation Training") and Chapter 43 ("Saxophone Pitch Tendency Guide") for more detailed information.

Pitch Is Flat Overall

1. Push the mouthpiece in on the neck cork if tuning pitches are flat.
2. If high register is flat, check voicing. The tongue should be in "hee" position.
3. Be sure embouchure is not loose.

Pitch Is Sharp Overall

1. Pull the mouthpiece out on the neck cork if tuning pitches are sharp.
2. If the high register is sharp, check voicing. Generally, pitch can be lowered by pushing the arch of the tongue slightly forward and/or by creating space in the throat or larynx while the tongue stays in the "hee" position (see Chapter 33).
3. Be sure embouchure is not too tight.

Issues Related to Articulation

See Chapter 9 ("AIR-ticulation") and Chapter 28 ("Articulation") for more detailed information.

Very Heavy, Slappy, Harsh

1. The player may be tonguing with the syllable "TAH," which puts too much tongue in contact with the reed and results in a heavy downward motion underneath the reed.
2. Use the "DOO" syllable instead. The motion of the tongue is back, away from the reed, rather than down under the reed.

Squeaks Occur When Tonguing

Remember that squeaks indicate some kind of imbalance with the vibration of the reed.

1. The student may be moving their embouchure along with the movement of the tongue. Embouchure should not change when tonguing.
2. The student may be squeezing the embouchure when moving the tongue to articulate.
3. Proper tongue position is not being used.
   - The back of tongue should stay up by the inside of the back molars in the "hee" position.
   - The spot used on the tongue should be on the top of the tongue, about a half-inch back from the tip.
   - The tongue should be contacting the very tip of the reed. It is common for students to try touching the flat part of the reed for articulation and this will lead to articulation problems.
   - Be sure the student is using the "DOO" syllable rather than "TAH" (see the explanation in the previous section).
4. See the suggestions listed previously in the "Issues Related to Tone: Squeaks in the sound" section.

Notes Sound Clipped/Too Short

The student is stopping the sound by placing their tongue back on the reed (as in "DOOT") rather than using an air release (as in "DOO").

Pop Tonguing (Notes Sound Slapped)

1. Too much tongue is contacting the reed, and the tongue is moving in a downward motion.
2. The student needs to use "DOO" syllable and support the sound with air.

Lethargic and Undefined, Slow

1. This may be caused by an approach called *anchor tonguing*, which occurs when the tip of the tongue stays in contact with the lower lip/teeth and the player is using a spot too far back on the tongue to articulate. The motion is up and down, and it is very restricted.
2. To fix anchor tonguing, work with the student on over-correcting by emphasizing the tip-of-tongue to tip-of-reed contact until you are certain that they are no longer anchoring the tip of the tongue on the lower lip/teeth. Then reinforce the fundamental concepts of articulation with the proper contact points (a spot about a half-inch back from tip of tongue contacts tip of reed).

Issues Related to Extraneous Sounds

Blips Between Notes (Tongue/Finger Coordination Issue)

1. Have the student play the passage slowly and slurred to observe if fingers are moving together as they raise and lower keys.
2. Once the finger technique is correct, keep the tempo slow and add in the tongued articulations. Slowly increase speed.

Air Leak (Hissing Sound) in Tone

Embouchure is not sealing around the mouthpiece and air is escaping.

Clicks On the Instrument

A felt or cork is missing, and metal is hitting metal. Listen carefully to find the source of the sound and find out where the contact is happening.

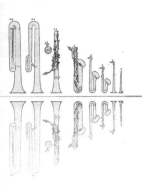

Reminder: Once the player has tuned and placed the saxophone mouthpiece in the optimal position, they will still need to compensate for notes that have an acoustical tendency to be sharp or flat. This is primarily done through voicing while maintaining proper air support and embouchure.

As a general suggestion, pitch can be lowered by pushing the arch of the tongue slightly forward (see the section on "Mouthpiece Flexibility" in Chapter 33, "Intonation Training") and/or by creating space in the throat or larynx while the tongue stays in the "hee" position. Because the tongue and throat are connected, movement of the tongue will change the shape of the throat, and changes in the shape of the throat will result in tongue movement. There are varying opinions among saxophonists on where the focus should be placed when lowering pitch: whether it should be on the movement of the tongue or the shape of throat. We believe there's an inherent connection and that these principles work together in lowering pitch and finding the ideal resonance for any given note.

When pitch is flat, check that the tongue is in the "hee" position, embouchure is not too loose, and correct air support is being used. If all those components are in place, the only way to raise a pitch is by opening another key as a vent.

Common Pitch Tendencies on Most Saxophones

Palm Keys: – often sharp

High A, B, C, C♯: – often sharp

Middle D and E: – sharp

Middle C♯ (middle of staff): – flat!

Low B♭ -- sharp

The following section includes many corrective fingering suggestions. *Keep in mind that these corrections do not replace regular fingerings and should only be used on long, sustained notes where the tuning correction is vital, and where finger work is easy to maneuver.* Students should always keep working to improve voicing, air support, and embouchure in pursuit of establishing correct intonation.

Playing & Teaching the Saxophone. Allison D. Adams and Brian R. Horner, Oxford University Press. © Oxford University Press 2023.
DOI: 10.1093/oso/9780197627594.003.0043

Palm Keys (Often Sharp)

- If a honking, low sound comes out, the embouchure is probably too loose, or the reed may be too soft.
- Tight embouchure is common on high notes and will make pitch sharper—embouchure should be firm but not squeezed.
- As discussed in the Palm Keys chapter (Chapter 22), players often fail to support their air when playing these notes. This will cause pitch to be sharp.
- On Palm D, students can add the right-hand index finger to lower pitch. You can use this on Palm E♭ as well, but it becomes less effective as the palm key notes go higher.
- Palm E, F, and F♯ will be rarely used in high school band literature. In solo work, students should work on finding the correct voicing, air support, and embouchure to play these notes in tune.

High A, B, C, C♯ (Often Sharp)

- On high A, you can add the right-hand index finger to lower pitch.
- On high B, there's not much you can do through finger correction because the addition of the right-hand index finger will change the note to B♭.
- On high C and C♯, you can add the right-hand index finger to help lower pitch if needed.

Middle D and E (Sharp)

- You can have students push down the low B♭ or low B key while they play middle D or E to help lower the pitch. The low B♭ key will lower the pitch to a greater extent.

Middle C♯ (Flat)

Because no keys are depressed for middle C♯, it often feels exposed and ugly. Students must learn how to use their voicing and air to find the best tone on this note.

- Air must be supported, but not overblown.
- Students should not "bite up" on the reed to try to bring up pitch.
- On some brands of saxophone, you can play this note using the left-hand ring finger and the octave key. This brings pitch up significantly (sometimes too much), but it should mainly be applied to sustained notes. Sometimes this fingering is ok to use in faster passages that bridge C♯ to the middle register.
- Another trick to raise pitch is to play C♯ and open up the side B♭ key or the side C key.

Low B♭ (Sharp)

This note is always sharp but, fortunately, is rarely used in high school band literature. The only way to correct pitch on this note is to place a small, circular "saxophone mute" in the bell.

SAXOPHONE EQUIPMENT

The saxophone itself has a lot of moving parts and there is a lot of gear that goes along with it—mouthpiece, reed, ligature, neck strap. Three professional players may each have a different opinion about which brands are best. We both endorse Selmer (Paris) saxophones and D'Addario Woodwinds reeds, but we are going to present recommendations across the five mainstream brands of saxophones and three mainstream brands of reeds.

As a player progresses, they will need to upgrade their equipment to reach their potential. This can be done in small steps, as some of the less expensive purchases will make a big difference in their musical growth.

Suggested order of upgrades:

1. Reeds

   Although not an equipment upgrade, reed strengths will be increased periodically in consultation with the instructor.

2. Neck strap

   The stock neck strap is often uncomfortable and flimsy. A more comfortable one should be purchased as soon as possible.

3. Mouthpiece

   Stock mouthpieces are not very consistent, and this upgrade will make a big difference in improved tone and response. Ideally, a mouthpiece should be upgraded after a few years of playing. For a band director, the purchase of professional mouthpieces will have a dramatic effect on the band's saxophone section!

4. Ligature

   Once a professional-level mouthpiece has been obtained, a new ligature will improve the consistency of how the reed is held on the mouthpiece. This improves tone and response.

5. Saxophone

   Upgrading to a higher-quality instrument will improve tone, response, and technical facility. This is a major purchase and should be done in consultation with an instructor.

Reeds

The saxophone's sound is produced when air passes through the reed and causes its fibers to vibrate. Therefore, the strength and quality of a reed will greatly impact the sound of a saxophone and the ease with which it plays.

Playing & Teaching the Saxophone. Allison D. Adams and Brian R. Horner, Oxford University Press. © Oxford University Press 2023.
DOI: 10.1093/oso/9780197627594.003.0044

Reeds are classified and numbered according to their *strength* (stiffness)—the lower the number, the softer and easier-blowing the reed, and vice versa. The numbers are often (and mistakenly) referred to as "sizes."

As a very general rule, beginner players start with reed strength 2 and progress to a 3 or 3.5 as they improve. There can be significant variation; for example, a professional player may never use a reed harder than a 3 and increases beyond 3.5 are rare. This largely depends on the mouthpiece being used and the type of music being played rather than someone's playing ability.

Beginners

Start with reed strength 2 for a young beginner student who has not yet developed the muscles necessary to support the embouchure. Within a year the student should move to a 2.5 reed, and once those muscles are strengthened further, the student will be able to move up to 3.

Recommended brands:

- D'Addario Woodwinds Reserve
- Vandoren Traditional
- Rico. The basic bulk box of Rico reeds is not as high quality and does not sound as good, but they are cheaper and may be a good solution for a young player who breaks a lot of reeds. In this case, suggest they upgrade to a higher quality reed by the end of their first year.

Intermediate

- D'Addario Woodwinds Reserve, 3 or 3.0+
- Vandoren Traditional strength, 3

High School and Beyond

- D'Addario Woodwinds Reserve, 3.0+ or 3.5
- Vandoren Traditional, 3 or 3.5

Synthetic Reeds

Synthetic reeds are becoming increasingly common and higher in quality. However, at the time of this writing, they don't produce the same warmth and expressiveness of tone as a cane reed. They are highly durable and can be a great choice for baritone saxophone, tenor saxophone, and general use in marching band.

Neck Straps

When choosing a neck strap, consider the points below:

1. There should be no elastic in the neck strap—the neck strap should not bounce. Bouncing creates extra stress on the vertebrae and can lead to poor posture and back pain.

2. The neck strap should have a clasp that closes the hook so that it won't come unhooked. This unfortunate event has led many saxophones to their demise!

3. Choose a neck strap that has some padding around the back of the neck for comfort.

Mouthpieces

All beginner saxophones will come with a mouthpiece in the case. Some of these (accompanying any of the mainstream brands) may be perfectly fine for the student to use at the outset. However, serious middle and high school students should upgrade their mouthpiece, if at all possible, to enable the greatest amount of progress with regard to tone production, intonation, and response.

Suggested mouthpieces (again, it is strongly recommended that you choose equipment in consultation with your teacher):

Classical/Wind Band

- Soprano saxophone: Vandoren Optimum SL3, Selmer S90 180, Selmer Concept
- Alto saxophone: Vandoren Optimum AL3, Selmer S90 190
- Tenor saxophone: Selmer S90 170
- Baritone saxophone: Selmer S90 190

Jazz

The exact size may vary from player to player. Keep trying different brands and sizes until you find one that is comfortable for the player.

Alto Saxophone

- Selmer S90, a great starting point for middle/high schoolers
- Hard rubber New York Meyer, size 6 may be a good one to try first
- D'Addario Select Jazz D6M
- Ted Klum
- Vandoren Java
- Jody Jazz Hard Rubber

Tenor Saxophone

- D'Addario Select Jazz D7
- Otto Link Tone Master
- Morgan Excalibur
- Bobby Dukoff
- Berg Larson
- Jody Jazz
- Ted Klum
- Navarro

Ligatures

As with mouthpieces, a ligature will be included in the case of the beginner's instrument and will, in most cases, be fine for them to use initially. Serious middle and high school students should upgrade their ligature. This can make a big difference in your student's ability to improve their tone and is not an expensive purchase.

1. Rovner Ligatures—Dark and Light ($24–50)
   - These ligatures are good for high school students because they are extremely durable.
   - Professional players often find that this ligature dampens the vibration of the reed too much.
     - If your student is producing a brighter, edgier tone and wants to make it darker, go with the Rovner Dark.
     - If your student is producing a darker, stuffier tone, have them try the Rovner Light.
2. D'Addario Woodwinds H-Ligature is a basic and simple ligature of higher quality than a stock ligature ($40–50)
3. There are many professional ligatures on the market, ranging from $100–250+. These brands are ever-changing and should be explored with the expertise of an instructor.

Saxophones

A general (and vitally important) piece of advice to students is to make purchases within these mainstream brands *in consultation with the instructor*. There are many other brands available, some of which claim to be "professional" instruments available at lower prices. However, because of the mechanics of the saxophone, a poor-quality instrument or reed can completely derail a young student. There are few situations more frustrating for both teacher, student, and parents than having spent money on a new instrument only to find out that it will not allow progress and needs to be replaced.

Mainstream Saxophone Brands

- Selmer
- Yamaha
- Yanagisawa
- Keilwerth
- P. Mauriat

Mainstream Reed Brands

- D'Addario Woodwinds
- Vandoren
- Legere (synthetic)

A Note About Used Instruments

The used saxophone market may present an opportunity for students to purchase a high-quality instrument on a more limited budget. High-quality saxophones can last many years and it is common to find used instruments available for sale that have been played for short periods of time. For example, if a player has a budget of $1,500 to upgrade their instrument, it may be a better strategy to purchase a used professional-level saxophone that is in good playing condition than to buy whatever new saxophone is attainable for that price. As always, it is very important for the student to involve their teacher in these purchasing decisions.

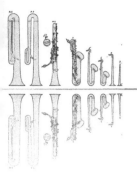

For the Student

Daily Maintenance

Cork grease

There is a cork on the end of the saxophone neck, and it is very important to keep the cork soft by applying cork grease frequently. This should be done every day when a saxophone is new, and anytime the cork feels dry. If the cork is not lubricated, it can crack and will need to be replaced by a repair technician.

Swabbing the body of the saxophone

This should be done at the end of every practice session.

1. Place the weight of the swab in the saxophone bell, letting it rest in the curve of the instrument. It is helpful to put the cloth in the bell as well.
2. Gently turn the saxophone upside down so that the weight drops out the smaller end of the saxophone tube.
3. Carefully pull the string until the swab comes out the smaller end of the saxophone.
4. Near the top of the instrument, there is a small rod that protrudes into the body of the saxophone. Be very careful that the swab does not get stuck on this rod.

Swabbing the neck of the saxophone

You must have either a neck brush, a silk swab, or a swab that is designed to fit the neck. Many basic swabs that are sold for the saxophone body are too thick to fit through the neck. It is a good idea to clean the neck and keep it dry; however, because there are no pads that will be affected by moisture in the neck, it is not as critical as swabbing the saxophone body.

Playing & Teaching the Saxophone. Allison D. Adams and Brian R. Horner, Oxford University Press. © Oxford University Press 2023.
DOI: 10.1093/oso/9780197627594.003.0045

Placing the saxophone in the case

There is a plastic cap or plug that should go in the top of the saxophone body when the body is resting in the case. When storing the mouthpiece in the case, students should leave the ligature on the mouthpiece and cover it with a plastic mouthpiece cap. This will keep the ligature from being bent and will protect the mouthpiece from getting scratched or chipped.

Cleaning the mouthpiece

This should be done once a week.

1. Take off the ligature and run the mouthpiece under cold water.
2. Use a gentle dish soap to lather the mouthpiece and then rinse it off.
3. Use a soft towel to pat the outside of the mouthpiece dry.
4. Do not use any brushes inside the mouthpiece, as this can scratch and damage the inside of the mouthpiece.
5. If you notice white calcium deposits around the tip of the mouthpiece, soak the tip of mouthpiece in a small cup of white vinegar for about ten minutes.

Screws

There are many screws on the saxophone that hold rods and keys in place. If you notice a screw is loose or coming out, use a small screwdriver (like those used for eyeglasses) to tighten it. Don't over-tighten! It is helpful to carry a small set of screwdrivers in the saxophone case.

Sticky pads

Pads become sticky over time due to condensation. The worst offenders are the G♯ key and the low C♯ key because they stay closed when the saxophone is at rest. The *bis* B♭ key can also be problematic.

Cigarette paper is the best material to use when cleaning a sticky pad. Paper money is often used in a pinch, but it should be avoided because the paper is dirty and can leave additional residue on pads. To clean a pad with cigarette paper:

1. Insert the cigarette paper between the pad and the tone hole.
2. Gently open and close the key, using a blotting method to clean the pad.

Avoid squeezing the pad down and pulling the paper out. This motion can cause damage to the pad itself. The paper trick is a quick fix, but if a pad continues to stick, take it to a repair shop. It may be time for the pad to be replaced.

Using key props, such as the product sold by Key Leaves, will allow pads to stay open as they dry and will greatly reduce sticking. Key Leaves also sells a spit sponge that can be used to dry pads before placing the horn in the case. These preventative measures will greatly reduce the problem of sticky pads.

Yearly maintenance

Take the saxophone to the local repair shop at least once a year. The repair person will check for pads that are not sealing and any other problems. After a year of playing, it is normal for some pads to need to be replaced.

You should not wait until there is a major problem to take your horn to a repair technician. Saxophones need yearly check-ups, just like people!

For the Band Director

The Saxophonist Survival Kit

Keep these materials on hand for maintenance and emergencies!

- Small screwdrivers
- Cigarette paper
- Crochet hooks of various sizes
- Felts and corks of various thicknesses and sizes
- Loctite Gel Control, or any type of superglue gel (also known as CA glue, standing for cyanoacrylate)
- Mini glue gun and glue sticks (from a craft store)
- Teflon tape
- Masking tape
- Pliers. Be sure to use smooth jaw pliers. Craft pliers are ideal.

If you want to purchase a pre-made repair kit for band directors, check out Ferree's Tools Emergency Repair Kit or J.L. Smith Repair Kits

Screws

Please see the discussion titled "Screws" earlier in this chapter.

Sticky Pads

Please see the discussion titled "Sticky Pads" earlier in this chapter.

Springs

Metal wires that sit in posts provide resistance for a key to open or close against so that it springs back into place after the note is played.

If a student has a floppy key that is not opening or closing correctly, look around to see if there is a metal wire sticking out somewhere. This is a spring that has popped out of the groove that holds it in place. Use one of the tools below to coax the wire back into the groove:

- Crochet hook (best option—keep one of these handy)
- Small screwdriver (careful not to scratch the saxophone)
- Plastic tip of a mechanical pencil

Felts and corks

There are many small pieces of felt or cork on the saxophone body. Occasionally, one of them will fall off, causing problems. It is a great idea to keep a supply of corks and felts of various thicknesses and sizes. Masking tape can also be used in a pinch when torn and shaped into the size of the missing felt or cork.

How will you know?

If a student's instrument is not working properly, look to see if you can determine which key is causing the problem. If it is not closing or opening correctly, determine if a felt or cork is missing. You can compare their saxophone to another one to help, but keep in mind that different brands may be constructed differently.

If you hear an annoying click, that is a sign that a cork/felt is missing or something is bent and hitting metal-on-metal.

To add a felt or cork:

- Make sure the surfaces are free from dirt or previous glue.
- Use a small amount of superglue gel to secure felt or cork in place. Test the instrument to make sure it works properly.

Pads

If a pad falls off, use a low temperature mini glue gun (the kind you buy at a craft store) to secure the pad back in place. Try to precisely line up the indented circle on the pad with the tone hole.

A pad must seal completely to work properly, and this must be done with a leak light, training, and care. You may be able to stick a pad back on the instrument to get a student through an emergency, but it needs to be taken to the repair shop as soon as possible so that an expert can make sure it is perfectly fitted.

Pearls

If a pearl falls off, use a small amount of superglue gel to secure the pearl back in place.

Neck Cork

If a neck cork cracks or becomes compressed, wrap teflon tape around the cork or neck to create a temporary "cork." Check the thickness by putting the mouthpiece on and making sure it goes down far enough for correct tuning placement.

When a neck cork compresses over time, it may become so thin that the saxophone mouthpiece wobbles. As a quick fix, you can also use regular copy paper to wrap the cork and build up the surface so that the mouthpiece is secure.

The neck should be taken to a repair shop to have the neck recorked as soon as possible.

Bent Octave Key on the Neck

It is very easy for the octave vent on the saxophone neck to become bent. This can happen if pressure is applied to the key when the neck is put on and off the body. If this happens, the key will not close correctly, and the saxophone will not work.

To fix:

- With the neck on the body, observe the contact between the body post and the neck mechanism. From this, you should be able to tell how it needs to be bent back in place.
- Take the neck off and gently hold the key down while using pressure to bend and adjust the metal loop around the bottom of the neck.
- Put the neck back on the body and see if the adjustment aligned the parts into proper contact.

Key Guards

These are the metal "cages" that sit over the large keys near the crook of the body and the bell. If pressure is applied to the key guards, they can be easily compressed down, causing keys to be stuck down or to not open correctly or fully. The E♭ key guard, located on the back of the crook at the bottom of the saxophone, is especially vulnerable.

To fix:

- Carefully bend the metal back in shape to the best of your ability.
- Due to the soft nature of the metal, you may be able to do this with your hands or by using something non-metal, like a drumstick, to give you leverage.
- You may not be able to make it look perfect (take it to the repair shop for that), but you can probably fix it to the point of being functional.

For the Repair Shop

Instruments should be taken to the repair shop at least once a year for a check-up, even if no problems are detected. Often, a student will become accustomed to leaks and other small inconsistencies and not even realize how they are affecting the horn. The student will be amazed to get the instrument back and find it easier to play!

Although a band director can help a student get through an emergency situation, these permanent repairs should be done only by a skilled repair person:

- Replace the pads.
- Remove the dents.
- Make permanent changes in felts and corks.
- Replace the neck cork.

46

▶ WELLNESS FOR THE YOUNG MUSICIAN

Music is a physical activity, similar to an athletic sport. Like athletes, musicians must take care of their minds and bodies. Just as sports teams have consistent training, drills, stretches, and mental preparation strategies, musicians too must follow a healthy regimen in these areas to perform successfully.

Consistent Practice = Quality over Quantity

Practice consistently, keeping in mind the priority of quality over quantity. It is better to practice thirty minutes every day than to cram for three hours once a week. Playing a musical instrument requires training small muscle groups, which can be easily injured with overuse. Practicing is also a mental discipline, requiring intense focus. Therefore, attention must be given to not only *what* you are playing, but *how* you are playing it. Any given practice session should take the body and mind into account, playing only as long as proper focus and proper use of the body can be maintained. For this reason, multiple short sessions often provide better results than long sessions in the practice room.

Typically, the minimum practice requirement for a college music major is about two hours per day. If you're considering a career in music, it is important to start building a healthy approach as soon as possible. For more detail, see Chapter 47, "Suggested Practice Routine and Warm-up".

Musical Drills = Fundamental Exercises

A football team can't walk on the field and win the game without first practicing basic drills and plays, which hone the players' skills and focus on specific elements of the game. Musicians should think of their practice sessions in the same way. It's important to isolate the individual skills needed to be a successful saxophonist and work on daily exercises that allow you to isolate and improve these skills. These skills should include long tones, overtones, exercises focused on vibrato/articulation/hand position, mouthpiece pitch, pitch bends, and scales.

For more detail, see Chapter 47, "Suggested Practice Routine and Warm-up."

Playing & Teaching the Saxophone. Allison D. Adams and Brian R. Horner, Oxford University Press. © Oxford University Press 2023.
DOI: 10.1093/oso/9780197627594.003.0046

Establish Proper Technique

Playing injuries and pain are very common among musicians, often the result of faulty technique or overuse. It is crucial to be aware of good posture, embouchure, and hand position to work toward healthy habits.

Tips

- Saxophone posture is particularly tricky because of the neck strap. Make sure the player sits or stands with good posture and adjusts the neck strap so that the saxophone mouthpiece comes to their mouth without requiring the head to move.
- The entire weight of the saxophone needs to rest on the neck strap, and the saxophone should lean against the body for balance. Always avoid resting the bottom of the saxophone on a chair. This is a common problem and negatively affects embouchure/neck position.
- The player should avoid holding the saxophone out in front of the body unless required for marching band formations. This puts unneeded tension on the hands and wrists, which could lead to tendonitis or carpal tunnel syndrome. Solo, concert band, and jazz pieces are often virtuosic and technical, so it's important to avoid strain on the hands and wrists.
- Review Chapter 10, "Saxophone Posture and Hand Position."
- Read the chapter on embouchure carefully and be sure to teach proper technique. However, if a student is struggling, consult with a saxophone specialist to help.
- Improper hand position is a common problem for students, and the importance of developing proper habits cannot be overstated. Fingers should look curved, much like the hand does naturally when resting. Avoid compressing knuckles to push down the keys, and keep fingers close to the pearls. This will require practice and training, but it will ultimately feel completely natural.
- Keep shoulders down and relaxed.

Stretches

Stretching for just a few minutes before a practice session can both help keep the body in good physical condition and focus the mind. Many saxophonists experience discomfort in the back, shoulders, forearms, and wrists, so preventative stretching is a wonderful habit to establish.

The stretches below target some of the muscle groups that are used frequently in playing the saxophone. For maximum benefit, pair each movement with an inhale or exhale through the nose, as marked in the descriptions.

Seated cat/seated cow

1. Inhale while rotating the bottom of the tailbone up and back to create a slight arch in the back. As the back arches, allow the gaze to shift upward.
2. Exhale while rotating the tailbone down and forward to create a curved spine. As the back curves, allow gaze to shift toward the belly button.
3. Repeat these steps for several breath cycles.

Arm stretch

Set-up: Hold the arms straight out, parallel to the floor with palms facing up.

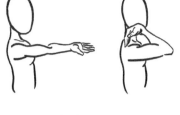

1. Inhale and stretch through the fingertips while keeping shoulders relaxed.
2. Exhale and bend the arms at the elbow and bring fingertips to touch the shoulders. The upper arms should stay parallel to the floor, and shoulders should stay relaxed.
3. Repeat these steps for several breath cycles.

Wrist bends: up and down

Set-up: Hold the arms straight out, parallel to the floor with palms facing down. Fingers should stretch forward with engagement and energy.

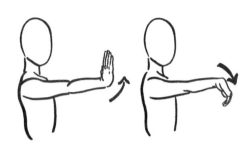

1. Inhale and bend the wrist, pointing the fingertips up to the ceiling while keeping the arms parallel to the floor.
2. Exhale and bend the wrist downward so that the fingertips point toward the floor.
3. Repeat these steps for several breath cycles.

Wrist rotation: side to side

Set-up: Hold the arms straight out, parallel to the floor with palms facing up. Fingers should stretch forward with engagement and energy.

1. Inhale and rotate the wrist to bring the pinky fingers toward one another while keeping the palms flat, as if there are dinner plates sitting on top of each hand. Keep the arms parallel to the floor.
2. Exhale and rotate the wrists to bring the pinky fingers away from each other while keeping the palms flat, as if they are still balancing the plates.
3. Repeat these steps for several breath cycles.

Chest opener: elbow touch

Set-up: Fingertips touch the shoulders, with elbows pointing out away from the torso.

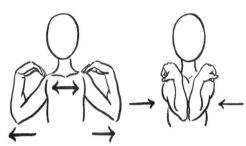

1. Inhale and push the elbows back to feel a stretch across the front of the chest.
2. Exhale and bring the elbows together to touch in front of the body while keeping fingertips on the shoulders. Try to keep the spine tall as you do this.
3. Repeat these steps for several breath cycles.

Chest opener: cactus arms

Set-up: Hold arms out to the sides and parallel to the floor. Bend the elbows to point the fingers up to the ceiling with palms facing forward.

1. Inhale and push the elbows back to feel a stretch across the front of the chest.
2. Exhale and rotate the shoulders to bring the fingertips pointing down to the ground, while maintaining the 90-degree angle of the arm.
3. Repeat these steps for several breath cycles.

Side stretch

Set-up: Bring the arms up overhead, interlace fingers and extend pointer fingers up, thumbs pointing behind.

1. Inhale and stretch arms up while keeping shoulders down.
2. Exhale and lean over to the right, stretching through the left side of the torso. While doing this, keep the hips in the same plane as the shoulders (avoid bending forward or leaning backwards with the hips).
3. Inhale and come back up to the center.
4. Exhale and lean over to the left, stretching through the right side of the torso. While doing this, keep the hips in the same plane as the shoulders (avoid bending forward or leaning backwards with the hips).
5. Inhale and return to the center.
6. Repeat these steps for several breath cycles.

Wall clock

Set-up: Stand about six inches from wall so that your right hip is closest to the wall and your feet are parallel to it. Imagine that a giant clock is drawn on the wall, with twelve o'clock straight up above your head. For this stretch, your arms will act as the "hands" of the clock. Be sure to listen to your body and move through the steps only as far as is comfortable!

1. Inhale and reach up and place the right palm against the surface of wall as high up as you can comfortably reach. Imagine that you are reaching up to "twelve o'clock."
2. Exhale and slide your right arm along the wall to "one o'clock" on the imaginary clock face.

3. Inhale and stretch your fingers further toward "one o'clock," as if reaching for the number.
4. Exhale and slide your right arm along the wall to "two o'clock."
5. Inhale and stretch your fingers further toward "two o'clock," as if reaching for the number.
6. Exhale and slide your right arm along the wall to "three o'clock."
7. Inhale and stretch your fingers further toward "three o'clock," and if it feels ok to do so, keep the pinky side of the hand against the wall while rotating the palm up to the ceiling. You may choose to stay here for a breath. Bring the palm back to the wall before moving to the next step.
8. Exhale and slide your right arm along the wall back up to "two-o'clock."
9. Inhale and stretch your fingers further toward "two-o'clock."
10. Exhale and slide your right arm along the wall up to "one o'clock."
11. Inhale and stretch your fingers further toward "one o'clock."
12. Exhale and slide your right arm along the wall up to "twelve o'clock."
13. Inhale and stretch your fingers further toward "twelve o'clock."
14. Exhale and release the arm, bringing it down and gently shaking it out.

Now turn around and repeat these steps using the left hand. As the left hand moves back, it will travel through "twelve o'clock, eleven o'clock, ten o'clock" and arrive at "nine o'clock" before moving back up.

Mental Preparation

Musicians spend a lot of time learning notes, rhythms, and articulations, but when it's time for the audition or the performance, it is often their mental focus that determines the outcome. Just like an athlete, a musician must prepare well, but also be able to deliver under pressure.

A technique that has been proven to help reduce anxiety and increase focus is intentional breathing. Slowing down the breath helps to calm the central nervous system, decreasing heart rate and increasing focus.

Measured Breathing

Before you start, decide which breath combination you want to use (see chart on next page). You might also want to set a timer with a gentle alarm, or put on a short song and do the exercise until the music ends.

1. Sit in a comfortable position and close your eyes. Let your hands rest on your lap.
2. Start breathing through the nose rather than the mouth. It is a bit easier to control the breath this way and has the added benefit of delivering warm air to the lungs.
3. Start your breath combination, counting in your head or following the direction of the leader. If your thoughts start to wander, gently refocus on the counts. Keep repeating the same combination until the end of your time, or until you choose to switch to a different combination.

Counting Combinations

Inhale	Pause and Hold	Exhale	Pause and Hold
4	0	4	0
4	1	8	4
6	1	8	4
1–8 Start at 1. Add one each cycle until you get to 8. Repeat 8 for a few cycles. Subtract one each cycle until you are back to 1.	1	Same as Inhale	1

Alternate Nostril Breathing

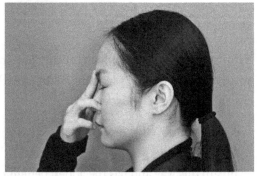

This is a great way to quiet anxiety and calm the nervous system, done by inhaling/exhaling through one nostril while closing the other off with a finger or thumb. Try it to help focus your mind before a performance!

1. Sit in a comfortable position.
2. Rest your left hand in your lap.

3. Bend the right arm at the elbow and gently allow your index and middle fingers to rest on your forehead, between your eyebrows.
4. Bring your right fingers to your nose, placing the thumb against the right nostril and the ring finger by the left nostril, just below the nasal bone.
5. Press the ring finger to close the left nostril.
6. Empty the lungs through your right nostril.
7. Inhale slowly, steadily, and deeply through the right nostril, filling your lungs completely while your left nostril is closed off.
8. Gently close your right nostril with the thumb and release the ring finger. Exhale slowly through the left nostril.
9. Now begin to inhale slowly and deeply through the left nostril, filling the lungs once again.
10. After inhaling completely, close the left nostril and begin to exhale through the right nostril.

You have now completed one cycle of Alternate Nostril Breathing (called Nadi Sodhana Pranayama in Yoga). Complete eight to ten cycles, or approximately four to five minutes.

Benefits

Blood receives more oxygen than in normal breathing, so one feels refreshed and the nerves are calmed. This also helps clear and focus the mind.

Overview of Common Wellness Approaches

There are several methods for approaching body mechanics and mental clarity that performers commonly find helpful, including Alexander Technique, Body Mapping, Feldenkrais, and Yoga. Here is a brief summary of each, along with some resources for future study.

Alexander Technique

The Alexander Technique is a method for bringing awareness to habitual movements that are inefficient or full of tension, and for cultivating a mindset of body awareness through correcting them. This method benefits anyone, but it can be essential when a musician is dealing with pain or a performance injury.

For more information:

- www.alexandertechnique.com
- Pedro De Alcantara, *Indirect Procedures: A Musicians Guide to the Alexander Technique*

Body Mapping

Body Mapping is an approach that educates students about proper kinesthetic movement. It is based on the premise that we each have a visual representation in our mind that directs how we move. Often, that map is inaccurate and leads to movement that is inefficient and can lead to injury. This approach uses self-observation, kinesthetic experience, and anatomical models to help students understand where changes need to be made. Developed by an Alexander Technique teacher, this approach shares many overlapping concepts.

For more information:

- www.bodymap.org
- Barbara Conable, *What Every Musician Needs to Know About the Body*

Feldenkrais

Feldenkrais is a method that uses movement sequences along with lessons in anatomy, physics, and human development to retrain the mind and develop proper physical movement. This retraining can reduce and prevent pain and injuries.

For more information:

- www.feldenkraisformusicians.com
- Moshe Feldenkrais, *Awareness Through Movement*

Yoga

Yoga is a practice of physical postures, breath control, and meditation that is derived from Hinduism but is now a mainstream form of exercise, meditation, and relaxation. It has been researched and proven that the practice of yoga can help reduce pain and performance anxiety in musicians. Yoga can help musicians learn to increase their focus and play in the present moment without concern for what has already been performed or is about to be performed in the music. The physical movements of yoga bring increased body awareness and can help establish proper habitual movement.

For more information:

- Mia Olson, *Musician's Yoga: A Guide to Practice, Performance, and Inspiration*

Overview of Common Injuries and Treatments

A staggering number of musicians report some level of performance injury at some point in their careers. While injuries can take many forms, here are the three of the most common ones:

1. *Carpal Tunnel Syndrome* is nerve compression in the wrist that can result in numbness or tingling in the hand and up the forearm. It is caused by repetitive motion over time and can also be caused by preexisting conditions such as rheumatoid arthritis or diabetes. Women are more likely to develop carpal tunnel than men because their wrists are often smaller. Common treatments include rest, stretching/strengthening exercises, anti-inflammatory drugs, and lifestyle changes. Surgery is an option when other treatments don't work.

2. *Focal Dystonia* is a task-specific neurological disorder in which muscles contract involuntarily. For saxophonists, this can occur in the lips, jaw, or fingers, and often results in uncontrollable shaking in one of those specific places when playing the instrument. The cause of this is unknown and there is no medical treatment. However, some musicians find wellness approaches such as Alexander Technique, Body Mapping, Feldenkrais, and Yoga to be effective roads to recovery.

3. *Tendonitis* is the inflammation of a tendon. For saxophonists, this often occurs in the wrist or forearm and can be caused by overuse and repetitive motion over time. Common treatments include ice/heat, rest, and over-the-counter pain medications.

SUGGESTED PRACTICE ROUTINE AND WARM-UPS

47

CONSISTENCY and QUALITY are more important than QUANTITY.

How Long Should I Practice?

The length of your practice sessions will vary depending on age and level, as you can see below. While it is important for students to dedicate substantial time and effort into the cultivation of their craft, many musicians fall into the trap of measuring their success by the quantity of practice time rather than quality. A student who keeps these sessions shorter, with specific goals and focus, will have more long-term success. When a student progresses to a level that requires more practice time, it becomes even more essential to divide these sessions, allowing the body and mind to rest.

1. Beginner student: twenty to thirty minutes per day, five days a week
2. Intermediate students: forty-five to sixty minutes per day, five to six days a week
3. Advanced high school student: one to two hours per day, six days a week
4. College music majors: two to three hours per day, six days a week

What Should I Practice?

- Stretch for one to two minutes
- Warm-up exercises to work on fundamental skills
- Scales
- Etudes and ensemble music
- Repertoire

How Should I Practice?

As with many tasks, just getting started is often the hardest part. Here are some tips to help you out!

1. If you can, have a consistent time during the day when you practice. When it's time, get your horn out and get started!

Playing & Teaching the Saxophone. Allison D. Adams and Brian R. Horner, Oxford University Press. © Oxford University Press 2023.
DOI: 10.1093/oso/9780197627594.003.0047

2. Have a plan for your practice session. Work with your teacher to establish a few stretches and warm-up exercises, and then do these every day. As you play these warm-ups, focus on your sound, physical movement, and use of air. *Really listen and notice how it feels to play.* Think of your warm-up as daily maintenance, like brushing your teeth, washing your hands, or taking a shower. They are important for personal health, and we do them over and over!

3. Use a tuner and a metronome. These are essential tools. Put the metronome on to help you play slow and steady, and to develop your internal pulse. Enjoy playing at a tempo where you feel calm and successful!

4. Play something fun every day to remind yourself why you love being a musician. However, make sure that you set a time limit on this and move on to working on newer skills that may be less appealing.

5. Work on new sections of music that are difficult! Don't avoid it just because it's hard or intimidating. Slow it down and break it into smaller passages. Listen actively so that you can evaluate your progress. Once you can play it perfectly at a slow tempo, increase the speed by five metronome clicks and play it again. Gradually build the small passages into larger sections. Talk to your teacher about how to do this. Learning how to practice things that are difficult is a skill that takes guidance and patience!

Warm-Up Routine

The purpose of warming up is to prepare the body and mind for the upcoming practice session. This is also a good time to work on exercises that isolate specific skills needed for musical success. For example, practicing long tones will help build endurance and tone. Articulation exercises will make it possible to play etudes and music more accurately. Vibrato exercises will help develop the physical skillset needed for musical expression.

The exercises needed to build a warm-up routine can be found throughout this book. Shown below is a sample that highlights some of the most important skills that an intermediate student should practice. The length and depth of a warm-up routine will vary based on the level of student and length of practice time.

1. Long tones.
   • Put a drone on tonic (Concert B♭ for alto/bari or Concert F for soprano/tenor) and play slowly, listening carefully for each interval to be in tune (no "waves").

2. Voicing and flexibility on the mouthpiece.
   - The musical notation below shows concert pitches used for the alto saxophone mouthpiece. The same exercises can be repeated on soprano, tenor, or baritone saxophone. Refer to mouthpiece pitches listed in Chapter 33, "Intonation Training," for each instrument. Practice these bends at a piano, matching each pitch as you go.

3. Overtones—Repetitive Overtone Voicing Routine (ROVR)
   F = fundamental
   1 = first overtone (octave)
   2 = second overtone (octave plus fifth)
   3 = third overtone (two octaves above fundamental)
   - Begin on low B♭. If the overtone on this pitch is too difficult, begin on the lowest note that produces a responsive overtone; however, continue to work on these problematic pitches.
   - Play four perfect repetitions using the syllable "KOO" to start the overtone.
   - Move up one chromatic pitch and perform four perfect repetitions. Continue to ascend until you can no longer produce a first overtone (strive to reach middle C♯).
     1. F → 1 (4x)

        Begin on low B♭. Ascend chromatically as high as possible.
     2. F → 2 (4x)

        1 → 2 (4x)

        Begin on low B♭. Ascend chromatically as high as possible.
     3. Optional integration of the third overtone:

        F → 3 (4x)

        1 → 3 (4x)

        2 → 3 (4x)

        Begin on low B♭. Ascend chromatically as high as possible.

4. Vibrato

- Begin with the metronome set at 60 BPM (beats per minute). When the motion is smooth and even, try out different keys and ranges. Once you have mastered that, increase tempo to 66 BPM, then 72 BPM, then 80 BPM. If these tempos feel too fast, start slower. It is essential that you master the correct motion before aiming for speed.

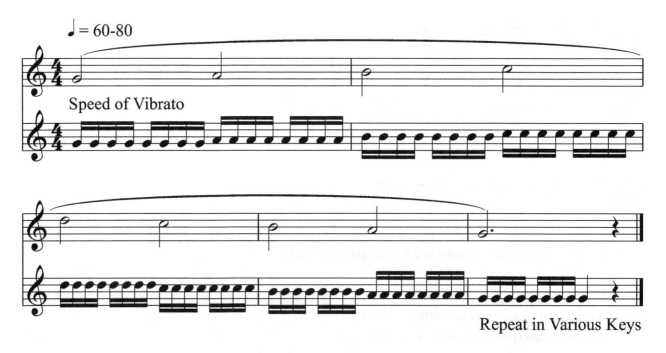

Repeat in Various Keys

5. Articulation

- Pick a tempo that challenges you but also allows you to play this cleanly and evenly with the metronome. Play this exercise on a few different scales!

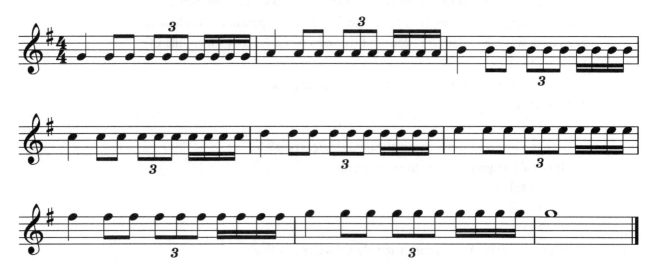

Hand Position

Start slowly, watching in the mirror for perfect hand position. Make sure fingers are curved, knuckles do not collapse, and fingers stay close to the pearls!

The examples below focus on low register hand position. Repeat these exercises for a week, building tempo and refining hand position. The next week, play them an octave higher. This kind of focused hand position work can also be done while playing scales at a slow tempo, or while isolating one measure or phrase from a piece of music.

Exercise 1

Exercise 2

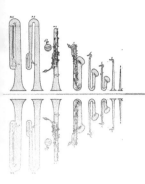
Listening

As discussed in the chapter on musicality (Chapter 35), listening to professional musicians is crucial to the development of tone and musicianship. Young saxophonists must be encouraged to listen to professional saxophonists in order to develop a proper concept of tone and to recognize the possibilities of the instrument.

Listed below are some of the historically significant classical saxophonists. As the level of performance increases each year, there are numerous emerging artists of note beyond the scope of this list. It is also important to note that the sound and approach to classical saxophone playing has changed over the years, and it continues to evolve. A good place to find high-level professional players is by searching the online rosters of endorsing artists for companies such as Conn-Selmer, Yamaha, D'Addario Woodwinds, and Vandoren.

Historically Significant Classical Saxophonists

Adolphe Sax
Rudy Wiedoeft
Marcel Mule
Cecil Leeson
Larry Teal
Sigurd Rascher
Daniel Deffayet
Jean-Marie Londeix
Eugene Rousseau
Frederick Hemke
Donald Sinta
Dale Underwood
Steven Mauk
Debra Richtmeyer
Claude Delangle
Marie-Bernadette Charrier
Nobuya Sugawa
Jean-Yves Fourmeau
Carrie Koffman

Playing & Teaching the Saxophone. Allison D. Adams and Brian R. Horner, Oxford University Press. © Oxford University Press 2023.
DOI: 10.1093/oso/9780197627594.003.0048

Chien-Kwan Lin
Otis Murphy
Kenneth Tse
Timothy McAllister

Repertoire

The saxophone has a vast body of repertoire that exceeds the scope of this book. It is ideal to have saxophone students working with a private saxophone instructor, who could then guide the player to the best repertoire for their level. As this is not always possible, the list below is a concise reference including some of the most standard pieces in the saxophone repertoire.

Classical

Etudes for high school students

F. W. Ferling, *48 Études*
H. Klose, *25 Daily Exercises for Saxophone* (arr. McAllister)
J. L. Small, *Twenty Seven Melodious & Rhythmical Exercises for Saxophone*
H. Voxman, *Selected Studies for Saxophone*

Standard solo repertoire for advanced middle school/high school level

J. S. Bach, *Arioso*
Eugene Bozza, *Aria*
Herbert Couf, *Introduction, Danse and Furioso*
Henri Eccles, *Sonata* (arr. Rascher)
J. F. Fasch, *Sonata* (arr. Rascher)
G. F. Handel, *Sonata No. 3* (arr. Rascher)
Pierre Lantier, *Sicilienne*
*Jeanine Rueff, *Chanson et Passepied*
Robert Schumann, *Three Romances* (arr. Hemke)

Standard solo repertoire for advanced high school/college level

Eugene Bozza, *Improvisation et Caprice*
Paul Creston, *Sonata*
Jules Demersseman, *The Carnival of Venice*
Alfred Desenclos, *Prelude, Cadence, et Finale*
Alexander Glazounov, *Concerto*
*Ida Gotkovsky, *Brillance*
Bernard Heiden, *Sonata*
Jacques Ibert, *Concertino da Camera*
*Paule Maurice, *Tableaux de Provence*
Darius Milhaud, *Scaramouche*
*William Grant Still, *Romance*

Contemporary repertoire for high school level

> *Alan Theisen (curator), *Anthology of New Music for Alto Saxophone*. This collection contains a wide variety of music at varying levels, from early high school to college level. It is a great starting point for students to explore new music and diverse composers.

*Indicates composer(s) from an underrepresented group

Jazz

Jamey Aebersold, Various books with play-along tracks

Jeff Coffin, *The Saxophone Book* (Vol. 1-3)

Jerry Coker, *Patterns For Jazz*

Lennie Niehaus, *Basic Jazz Conception for Saxophone* (various volumes)

Mike Steinel, *Building A Jazz Vocabulary*

Various, *Omnibook*; collections of transcriptions from various artists including Charlie Parker, John Coltrane, Sonny Rollins, Stan Getz, and others

Further Reading

Saxophone Pedagogy

Debra Richtmeyer, *The Richtmeyer Method for Saxophone Mastery, Vol. 1 & 2*

Eugene Rousseau, *Saxophone Artistry in Performance and Pedagogy*

Larry Teal, *The Art of Saxophone Playing*

Saxophone History

Richard Ingham, *Cambridge Companion to the Saxophone*

Paul Lindemeyer, *Celebrating the Saxophone*

Michael Segell, *The Devil's Horn*

Saxophone Voicing and Altissimo

Rosemary Lang, *Beginning Studies in the Altissimo Register*

Sigurd Rascher, *Top Tones*

Eugene Rousseau, *High Tones*

Donald Sinta, *Voicing*

Extended Techniques

Daniela Kientzy, *Les Sons Multiples Aux Saxophones*

Jean-Marie Londeix, *Hello! Mr. Sax, Parameters of the Saxophone*

Marcus Weiss, *Techniques of Saxophone Playing*

General

Barbara Conable, *What Every Musician Needs to Know About the Body: The Application of Body Mapping to Making Music*

Robin Fountain and Thomas Verrier, *The Ensemble Musician: Six Principles for a More Rewarding Life in Music*

Timothy Gallwey, *The Inner Game of Tennis*

Brian Horner, *Living The Dream (The Morning After Music School)*

Janet Horvath, *Playing (Less) Hurt: In Injury Prevention Guide for Musicians*

Victor Wooten, *The Music Lesson*

Now that you know all the chromatic notes, you can play any scale.
Practice these scales slurred and tongued.

C Major

G Major

F Major

D Major

B♭ Major

A Major

E♭ Major

E Major

A♭ Major

B Major

D♭ Major

F♯ Major

Chromatic Scale—Two Octaves

Transposition exercises are included across several chapters in the "Learning the Notes" section to teach this topic in a gradual and consistent way. This appendix consolidates the transposition exercises into one comprehensive resource, and it also includes additional transposition challenges.

The Saxophone Transposition Decoder

Can you read this statement?

____ ____ ____ ____ ____ ____ ____ ____ ____   ____ ____ ____ ____ ____

  No? Why not? You need a decoder, of course!! Use the information below to crack the code.

✌ = A   🏳 = P   ☝ = H   ☺ = K
👉 = E   ☠ = N   💧 = S   ✠ = X
🏳 = O   👍 = C   ☼ = R

  Transposing for different instruments is just like the example above: very confusing if you don't have a "decoder" memorized!

  Musicians often talk about transposing an instrument's key to "concert key." Concert key is a common reference that allows communication between members of an ensemble who are playing instruments that are pitched differently, such as the various saxophones.

  The four most common types of saxophone are soprano, alto, tenor, and baritone. These instruments are keyed in B♭ and E♭, as shown below. They all read music in the treble clef, and the fingerings are the same for each type of saxophone. Because they are in different keys, a C on soprano/tenor saxophone is a different concert pitch than a C on alto/baritone saxophone.

- B♭ Soprano Saxophone
- E♭ Alto Saxophone
- B♭ Tenor Saxophone
- E♭ Baritone Saxophone

To build your decoder, see how the pitches are placed on the staff to create a "Saxophone Transposition Decoder." Memorize this and use it to help you figure out the transposition for the exercises below.

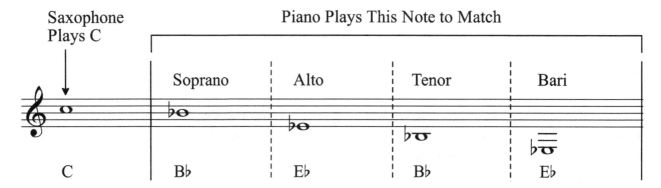

Decoder Version 2:

You may also find it helpful to view the decoder in a slightly different version. Use whichever makes more sense to you!

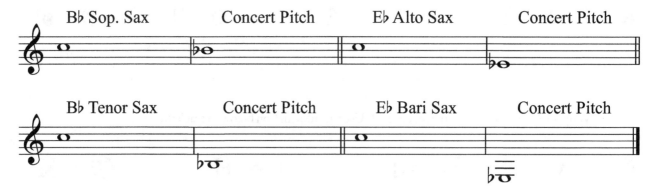

Now the fun begins, but it should be no problem for you now. Keep checking back to make sure your answers maintain the same intervallic relationship as your decoder!

Transposition Challenge 1 (Included in Chapter 17)

Using the staff above as your "decoder," fill in the missing notes below!

- HINT: The saxophone's written note on the staff will always be higher than the piano's written note (concert pitch). Why? That's easy! The saxophone is the best instrument so it's always on the top!!

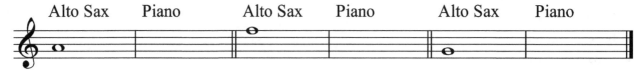

Transposition Challenge 2 (Included in Chapter 23)

As a beginning band teacher, ask your students to play a Concert B♭ scale. Fill in the decoder below and then figure out what scale your saxophone students need to finger to match the rest of the group!

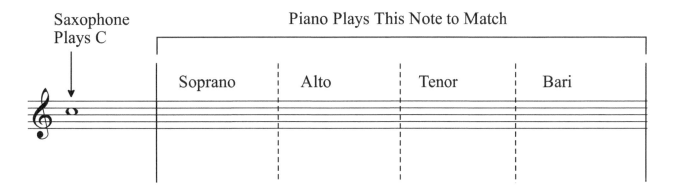

Concert Pitch: <u>B♭</u> <u>Major</u> <u>Scale</u>

Alto Saxophone: _____

Tenor Saxophone: _____

Baritone Saxophone: _____

Transposition Challenge 3 (Included in Chapter 25)

As a beginning band teacher, you would like your saxophone students to play "Mary Had a Little Lamb" together. Unfortunately, you must transpose it for them in order for it to work!

Fill in the decoder, and then use the staves below to transpose the first two bars of "Mary Had a Little Lamb" for your students so that they are playing the same pitches. Pick a range that would be easy to play for young students. It is acceptable for the saxophones to be playing in octaves rather than in unison.

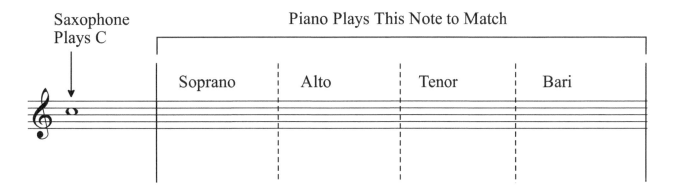

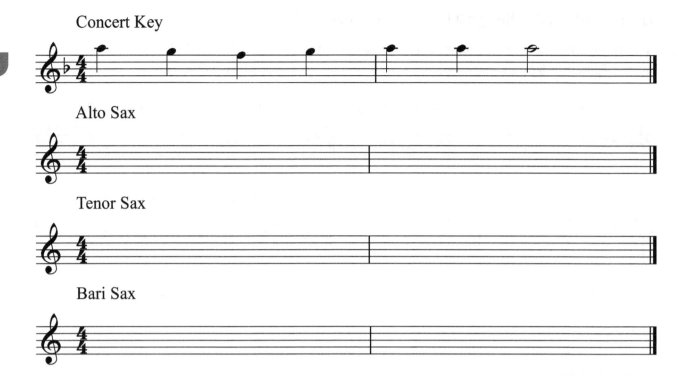

Concert Key

Alto Sax

Tenor Sax

Bari Sax

Transposition Challenge 4

In band rehearsal, you ask the students to play the following scales in concert key. Write in the scales your saxophone players will need to use to match the group!

TABLE B.1

Concert Key	Alto Saxophone	Tenor Saxophone	Baritone Saxophone
C			
B♭			
D			
G			

Transposition Challenge 5

A flute player and an alto saxophone player want to play a duet together for the Spring Showcase. They've chosen their music from a flute book. The flute is in concert key, just like a piano. Transpose the first four measures of the Flute 2 part for the saxophone player. Remember to choose the register that will work the best for the alto saxophone.

Sonata for 2 Flutes in F♯m, TWV 42:fis1 by Georg Philipp Telemann (1681–1767)

- Hint: A key that looks friendly for one instrument may not be so friendly when the music is transposed!

Transposition Challenge 6

A tenor saxophone player comes to you and asks if she can play "The Star-Spangled Banner" at the school basketball game along with her friend who plays alto saxophone. The alto player already has the music. Transpose the first phrase of the alto saxophone music so that the tenor saxophonist can play along.

The Star Spangled Banner (for Alto Saxophone)

The Star Spangled Banner (for Tenor Saxophone)

Blank Decoders

Feel free to copy the decoders below for transposition exercises as needed.

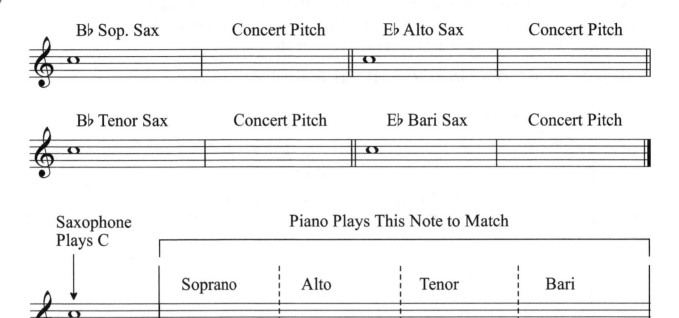

Transposition Answer Key

The Saxophone Transposition Decoder

| S | A | X | O | P | H | O | N | E | R | O | C | K | S! |

Transposition Challenge 1

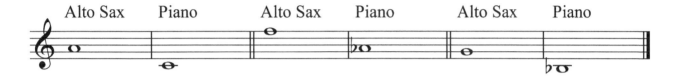

Transposition Challenge 2

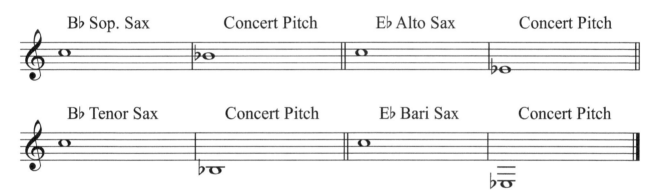

Concert Pitch: B♭ Major Scale
Alto Saxophone: G Major Scale
Tenor Saxophone: C Major Scale
Baritone Saxophone: G Major Scale

Transposition Challenge 3

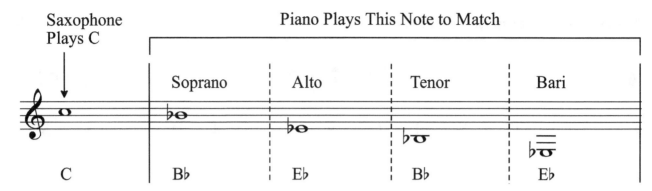

Mary Had a Little Lamb

Transposition Challenge 4

Concert Key	Alto Saxophone	Tenor Saxophone	Baritone Saxophone
C	A	D	A
B♭	G	C	G
D	B	E	B
G	E	A	E

Transposition Challenge 5

Sonata for 2 Flutes in F#m, TWV 42:fis1 by Georg Philipp Telemann—arranged for flute and alto saxophone

Transposition Challenge 6

The Star Spangled Banner (for Alto Saxophone)

The Star Spangled Banner (for Tenor Saxophone)

This Guide includes the following:

- Suggested Assignments
- Sample Rubric for Playing Assignments
- Quizzes
- Final Exam Ideas
- Sample Seven-Week Course Schedule

Suggested Assignments

Playing Assignments

Periodic playing assignments should be given to ensure that students are practicing regularly. This accountability helps students keep up with the assigned practice requirements.

It is suggested that playing assignments be chosen from the chapter covered two class periods before the due date. This gives students ample time to prepare. The rubric should be given to students in advance so that they understand the grading system.

The playing assignments should be recorded on video and turned in to the instructor on the due date. Students can record using their phones, but they should make sure that the frame includes both embouchure and fingers, and that they record with good lighting.

In this age of easily accessible technology, an interesting extension of the normal playing assignment is to have students record both parts of a duet and put them together using a program such as iMovie. This requires a student to keep a steady tempo on both parts, listen for tuning, and learn how to create simple virtual ensembles.

Take a Thirty-Minute Private Lesson

During the course of the methods class, it is extremely important for every student to take at least one private thirty-minute lesson, if possible, to help meet their individual needs. This can greatly assist a struggling student, as well as motivate a stronger student to tackle more advanced concepts. It is ideal if there is a graduate teaching assistant for the course who is able to take on the responsibility of teaching these lessons. Saxophone majors who are studying music education may also be able to teach these lessons, providing opportunities for them to practice saxophone pedagogy. This model may not work for every saxophone methods class.

Transposition

Transposition is a topic that is often overwhelming and confusing for students. To address this, small transposition exercises are sprinkled throughout the chapters in the "Learning the Notes" section. This approach allows students to absorb information in a friendlier way, building their skills week-to-week, and it helps the professor to address transposition consistently without consuming too much class time. Appendix B contains all the transposition exercises in one spot, and also offers additional challenges if time permits.

Teaching Demonstrations

In an instrument methods course, it is imperative that the instructor stay focused on the goal of training future educators of the instrument. To this end, it is important to include assignments that showcase a student's ability to not only play the instrument, but also to teach it. These assignments can take one of several forms, depending on the pace of the course and number of available class periods:

- Have students give live teaching demonstrations in class.
- Have students teach a "mock" beginner lesson outside of class to a peer who has never played the saxophone. This lesson can be recorded on video and submitted.
- Have students create video presentations on a specific topic, such as embouchure formation or hand position.

Sample Rubric for Playing Assignments

It is crucial that students understand how they will be graded on playing assignments before the first one is given. A clear rubric should always be given at least a week in advance of the due date. The instructor should let students know that they will be graded on accuracy of fingerings, articulation, and tempo. These are concrete concepts that can be improved through practice. Tone for the beginning player will develop throughout the course, but it is very important that a future teacher can model correct embouchure and use of air.

Playing assignments should consist of both scales and melodic playing. The instructor will need to modify the rubric to fit the assignment, but the rubric provided in this appendix can be used as a guide.

Suggested Playing Assignments

- *Playing Assignment #1*: G Major Scale, F Major Scale, tune taken from Chapter 17, "Zum Gali Gali" *or* "En Harmony" duet (if choosing the duet, take out grading "Posture" and replace with "Synchronization of Duet Parts").
- *Playing Assignment #2*: A Major Scale, E♭ Major Scale, tune taken from Chapter 19: "Shalom Chaverim," "Plouf Tizen Tizen," or "Gle(E)-Fully duet."
- *Playing Assignment #3*: E Major Scale, One-octave Chromatic Scale, tune taken from Chapter 22: "Barcarolle," "This Old Man," "German Dance," *or* "B♭ Blues Jam!" duet.
- *Final Playing Assignment*: Two-octave Chromatic Scale, A♭ Major Scale, tune taken from Chapter 26: "A New Season" by Darius Edwards, or a duet from Appendix D: Chamber Music.

If the course is shared with another instrument (for example, seven weeks of saxophone instruction and seven weeks of flute instruction) the final playing exam for the class can be a duet between the two instruments, combined using software such as iMovie.

Sample Rubric

	Accuracy of Notes/Fingerings (5 points)	Accuracy of Articulation (5 points)	Tone Quality (5 points)	Hand Position and Posture (5 points)	Total
Scale 1 (articulated)					20
Scale 2 (slur every four notes)					20

	Tempo (10 pts)	Rhythm (10 pts)	Notes and Fingerings (10 pts)	Articulation (10 pts)	Tone Quality (10 pts)	Posture (10 pts)	Total
Melody							60

Quizzes

It will be helpful for the progress of the students if you give two or three short quizzes throughout the course, asking them to demonstrate their knowledge of concrete concepts. This could include naming the parts of the saxophone, explaining the steps to forming embouchure and establishing correct voicing, naming solutions to common problems, etc. These quizzes should help students prepare for a written final (if one will be given) without consuming too much instructional time. Quizzes could also be given as "take-home" assignments if the instructor prefers. Suggested class periods and topics for quizzes are included on the sample schedule at the end of this appendix.

Final Exam Ideas (Non-Playing)

In addition to a final playing exam, the "written" final exam for this course could take various forms. A traditional written exam could cover important concepts from the semester, such as the basic components of embouchure, saxophone voicing, fingerings, posture, hand position, solutions to common problems, maintenance, etc. Alternately, a project such as a teaching demonstration or pedagogy presentation could be assigned and due on the final exam date.

Sample Seven-Week Course Schedule

It would be impossible to cover every detail in this book during a seven-week saxophone methods course. The goal is to progress through the "Getting Started" and "Learning the Notes" sections, while covering as many of the "In-Depth" chapters as time allows and familiarizing students with the resources offered in "Teaching Tools." The professor will need to modify this to fit the schedule and needs of their individual class. Once students have a solid foundation of saxophone fundamentals, they should be able to utilize the remainder of this book as a resource in their future band room.

The first two class periods will cover many chapters. Although this may seem like a lot, remember that you will continue to reinforce these important basic skills in the classes to come. For example, students should understand a concept, such as embouchure, on the first day, but they may not be able to successfully demonstrate it until they have had time to experience it through practice.

Each class period should begin with a review of the chapter that was assigned as practice material. This can be used as the warm-up, and you can continue reinforcing basic concepts such as posture, voicing, embouchure formation, breathing, etc.

Class	Topics Covered
Class #1	**Chapters 1-9** Instructional Focus: • Parts of the Saxophone (Chapter 2) • Assembly and Disassembly of neck/mouthpiece/reed—*not entire horn yet* (Chapters 3-4) • First sounds (Chapters 5-8) Playing Focus: • AIR-ticulation (Chapter 9) Student Assignment for Next Class: • Read and review Chapters 1-8 • Practice Chapter 9, AIR-ticulation
Class #2	**Chapters 3-4, 10, 13, 41** Instructional Focus: • Assembly and Disassembly of Saxophone Body (Chapters 3-4) • Posture and Hand Position (Chapter 10) Playing Focus: • The First Notes: BAG FED (Chapter 13) Student Assignment for Next Class: • Read Chapter 41, First Lesson Planning Guide • Practice Chapter 13, The First Notes BAG FED
Class #3	**Chapters 11-12, 14-15** Instructional Focus: • Basic Tuning (Chapter 11) • The Saxophone Family (Chapter 12) Playing Focus: • Middle C and Low C (Chapter 14) • Voicing and Overtones for Low Notes (Chapter 15) Major Scales: • C Major Student Assignment for Next Class: • Practice Chapter 14, Middle C and Low C • Practice Chapter 15, Voicing and Overtones for Low Notes

Class #4	**Chapter 16** Instructional Focus: • Review saxophone assembly by having students teach it to each other in pairs Playing Focus: • The Octave Key (Chapter 16) Student Assignment for Next Class: • Read Chapter 42, Troubleshooting • Practice Chapter 16, The Octave Key
Class #5	**Chapters 17, 28** Instructional Focus: • Quiz #1: Fingerings, Embouchure, Voicing • Articulation (Chapter 28) Playing Focus: • New Notes: F♯, C♯, B♭ (Chapter 17) • Introduce Playing Assignment #1 (due in Class #7) Major Scales: • G, D, F Student Assignment for Next Class: • Practice Chapter 17, New Notes: F♯, C♯, B♭ • Practice Playing Assignment #1 (due in Class #7)
Class #6	**Chapter 18-19** Instructional Focus: • Hand position through Flawless Fingers (Chapter 18) Playing Focus: • Low C♯, Low D♯, and G♯ (Chapter 19) Major Scales: • A, E, B♭, E♭, A♭ Student Assignment for Next Class: • Practice Chapter 19, Low C♯, Low D♯, and G♯ • Read Chapter 33, Intonation Training and Chapter 43, Saxophone Pitch Tendency Guide • Playing Assignment #1 due next class

Class #7	**Chapters 20, 33, 43**	**Playing Assignment #1 Due**
	Instructional Focus: • Intonation Training and Saxophone Pitch Tendency Guide (Chapters 33, 43) Playing Focus: • One Octave Chromatic Scale (Chapter 20) • Introduce Playing Assignment #2 (due in Class #9) Scale: • Chromatic Scale, One Octave (from low C to middle C) Student Assignment for Next Class: • Practice Chapter 20, Filling in the Gaps: One Octave Chromatic Scale • Practice Playing Assignment #2 (due in Class #9) • Read Chapter 37, Soprano, Tenor, and Baritone Saxophone	
Class #8	**Chapters 21, 37**	
	Instructional Focus: • Quiz #2: Fingerings, Articulation, Common Problems • Soprano, Tenor, and Baritone Saxophone (chapter 37) Playing Focus: • Second Octave Chromatic Scale (chapter 21) Scale: • Two Octave Chromatic Scale (from low C to high C) Student Assignment for Next Class: • Practice Chapter 21, Chromatic Scale: Second Octave • Playing Assignment #2 due next class	
Class #9	**Chapters 22-23, 45**	**Playing Assignment #2 Due**
	Instructional Focus: • Saxophone Maintenance (Chapter 45) Playing Focus: • Review Chromatic Scales • Palm Keys (Chapter 22) • Low B and B♭ (Chapter 23) • Introduce Playing Assignment #3 (due in Class #11) Student Assignment for Next Class: • Read Chapter 44, Saxophone Equipment • Practice Chapter 22, Palm Keys • Practice Chapter 23, The Lowest Notes: B♭ and B • Practice Playing Assignment #3 (due in Class #11)	

224

Class #10	**Chapters 24-25**	

	Instructional Focus:
	   • Quiz #3: Fingerings, Tuning, Common Problems
	
	Playing Focus:
	   • Alternate Fingerings for B♭ (Chapter 24)
	   • Alternate Fingerings for F♯ and C (Chapter 25)
	
	Scale:
	   • Full-range Chromatic Scale with chromatic fingerings
	
	Student Assignment for Next Class:
	   • Practice Chapter 24, The Many Fingerings of B♭
	   • Practice Chapter 25, Alternate Fingerings for F♯ and C
	   • Playing Assignment #3 due next class	

Class #11	**Chapters 29-30**	**Playing Assignment #3 due** **Private lesson must be complete**

	Instructional Focus:
	   • Vibrato (Chapter 29)
	   • Voicing: The First Overtone (Chapter 30)
	
	Playing Focus:
	   • Introduce Final Playing Assignment
	   • Review Full-range Chromatic Scale
	
	Student Assignment for Next Class:
	   • Read Chapter 48, Saxophone Resource Guide
	   • Practice Final Playing Assignment	

Class #12	**Chapters 38-39, 47**	

	Instructional Focus:
	   • Altissimo Register (Chapter 38)
	   • Extended Techniques (Chapter 39)
	   • Saxophone Resources (Chapter 48)
	
	Playing Focus:
	   • Chamber Music (Appendix D)
	   • Review Full-range Chromatic Scale
	   • Final Playing Assignment
	
	Student Assignment for Next Class:
	   • Practice Final Playing Assignment	

Class #13	**Chapters 41-42** Instructional Focus: <ul><li>Review for Final Exam</li></ul> Playing Focus <ul><li>Chamber Music</li><li>Review Full-range Chromatic Scale</li></ul>
Class #14	**FINAL EXAM**

APPENDIX D **CHAMBER MUSIC**

Playing chamber music is a fun way to develop important skills such as tuning, blend, rhythm, and musical communication. The following examples are created for like-instruments (all E♭ saxophones or all B♭ saxophones, etc.) and can be used as supplemental musical examples.

Banaha

Kiluba Folk Song

Mòlìhuā

Chinese Folk Song

Jan Pierewiet

South African
Barn Dance Song

Burung Kakatua

Baha Indonesia
Children's Song

Herzliebster Jesu, was has du verbrochen

Johann Sebastian Bach

Wo Gott der Herr nicht bei uns hält

Johann Sebastian Bach

Wo Gott der Herr nicht bei uns hält

Johann Sebastian Bach

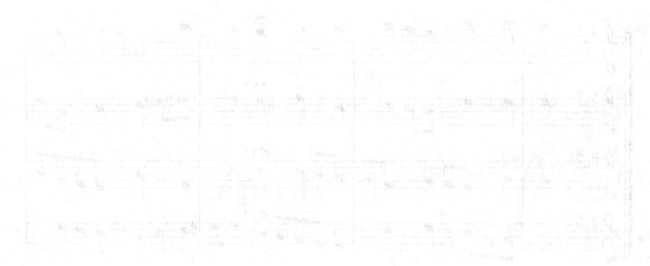

Acknowledgements

The authors would like to thank:

The people who taught us to play and teach the saxophone: Donald Sinta, Eugene Rousseau, Timothy McAllister, Steven Mauk, Denis Solee, Joe Dragone, Tom Ellison, Michael Crumb, Dan MacPherson, Tom Ives, Paul Tobler, and all the other teachers and band directors that pointed us in the right direction.

Michelle Chen, Phillipa Clubbs, Egle Zigaite, Jessie Coffey, and the team at Oxford University Press for believing in this book and helping us to bring it into the world.

Our students, past and present—as they say, we learn as much from you as you do from us.

The companies that support our work and make great equipment to help us do what we do: Conn-Selmer, D'Addario Woodwinds, Hercules Stands, Rush's Music, Lundsford's Music, Bailey's Band Room, and Consistent-C Winds.

Our colleagues, who offered input and support as we've written: Jeff Coffin, Tim McAllister, Don Sinta, Greg Tardy, Eugene Rousseau, Steven Mauk, Kenneth Tse, Carrie Koffman, Miles Osland, Victor Chavez, Maria Castillo, David Royse, Scott Campbell, Kristen McKeon, Jalissa Gascho.

The University of Tennessee-Knoxville Woodwind Methods II classes; Carrie Anderson, the Marietta Sixth Grade Academy band director, and her Class of 2026 saxophonists. Thank you for letting us test our "voicing-for-beginners" theories on you!

The University of Tennessee-Knoxville Saxophone Studio, for your modeling, as seen throughout the book, and for the various ways in which you served as our guinea pigs.

Eric Retterer, for your generous help with our video and recording sessions.

Corey Martin, UT Saxophone Graduate Teaching Assistant 2018–2020, for helping lay much of the groundwork on musical notation and first draft chapters for this book during your time at UT.

Our book's "Composer-in-Residence," Darius Edwards, for writing the original duets and final solo for the method, and for performing on the duet recordings as well. Your talent and passion will take you far!

Ariel Williams, UT Saxophone Graduate Teaching Assistant 2020–2022, for your feedback and an enormous amount of administrative support. Your tireless work on creating the music notation and computer images throughout the book was invaluable—we couldn't have pulled this off without you.

Timothy McAllister, for your generous foreword and your guidance and leadership over the years, to us personally and to the field generally.

Our de facto editor and illustrator, Jared Adams—thank you so much for your objective perspective and your humor. This book is much better for your enormous efforts.

Our parents, for supporting us from the beginning.

Our spouses and children—you've heard more discussion of saxophone over the last two years than you probably ever wanted to, and we appreciate your patience!

About the Authors

Dr. Allison Adams is Associate Professor of Saxophone at the University of Tennessee-Knoxville. An avid performer, she is also a member of the Estrella Consort Saxophone Quartet and the nief-norf Contemporary Music Ensemble. Adams frequently performs with the Knoxville Symphony and has presented lectures and recitals at the World Saxophone Congress, International Saxophone Symposium, NASA Conferences, and the International Clarinet Association Conference.

In addition to a fascination with saxophone pedagogy, Adams' research centers around performance injuries, wellness for musicians, and the integration of yoga into music performance. A chapter on her recovery from focal dystonia is available in the collection *Notes of Hope*, published by Mountain Peak Music. She has also authored an essay on yoga for musicians, which can be found in the multi-media resource *Cross Training for Musicians* (also available through Mountain Peak Music). She has taught several "Yoga for Musicians" courses for students ranging from high school to college. Her focus on wellness has also expanded to include presentations on the anatomy of breathing and how pregnancy affects saxophone performance.

Adams has previously served on the faculties of Ithaca College and Cornell University. She holds a B.M. in Music Education and Performance from Ithaca College, a M.M. in Music Performance from the University of Minnesota, and a D.M.A. from Arizona State University. Her main saxophone teachers have included Steven Mauk, Eugene Rousseau, and Timothy McAllister. Adams is a D'Addario Woodwinds Performing Artist, endorsing D'Addario Reserve reeds, and a Conn-Selmer Artist, endorsing Selmer (Paris) saxophones. She lives in Knoxville with her husband and three children. For more information, please go to www.allisondadams.com.

Brian Horner has designed a multifaceted career as a saxophonist, educator, artist manager, author, and entrepreneur. A graduate of the University of Michigan School of Music where he studied with Donald Sinta, his fifteen-year university teaching career has included appointments at Middle Tennessee State University, Austin Peay State University, the University of Tennessee, and Western Kentucky University. Horner has appeared at Carnegie Hall's Weill Recital Hall, Steinway Hall, and New York City's Mannes College of Music, as well as at the Glimmerglass Opera's Young Artist recital series in Cooperstown, NY, and has performed with the Nashville Symphony, the Nashville Chamber Orchestra, and the Gateway Chamber Orchestra. He has premiered more than a dozen new works for saxophone, and his recordings with pianist Elizabeth Avery include *Saxophone Music of M. Zachary Johnson—Live At Steinway Hall* and *Serenade—Music for Saxophone & Piano*, and garnered a cover feature in *Saxophone Journal*.

Horner is the owner of Sound Artist Support, is CEO/CCO of Craft Brewed Music˚, "the small batch streaming app," co-hosts *The Craft Brewed Music Podcast* with his longtime musical collaborator, Aaron Stayman, and has authored a series of books for Kendall Hunt Publishing: *Living The Dream . . . The Morning After Music School, Living The Dream . . . The Morning After Drama School* (with David Alford), and *Living The Dream . . . The Morning After Art School* (with John Watson). He presents music business and entrepreneurship lectures and saxophone clinics at colleges and conservatories around the country.

Brian Horner is a D'Addario Woodwinds Performing Artist, endorsing D'Addario Reserve reeds, a Conn-Selmer Artist, endorsing Selmer (Paris) saxophones, and endorses Hercules stands. He lives in Atlanta with his wife and daughter. For more information, please visit brianhornermusic.com.

About the Composer

Darius Edwards is a saxophonist and composer from Nashville, Tennessee. He graduated from the University of Tennessee-Knoxville with a bachelor's degree in music education with an emphasis in saxophone performance and a minor in music composition. As a performer, Edwards was named a winner in the 2020 University of Tennessee School of Music Concerto Competition, the 2019 Knoxville Music Study Club Scholarship Competition, and has been invited to perform at the International Saxophone Symposium hosted by the U.S. Navy Band. As a composer, Edwards' premieres include works for saxophone and piano, saxophone quartet, saxophone ensemble, and wind ensemble. His piece for wind ensemble, "Metropolis Downpour", is published by Murphy Music Press. In addition, his works have been selected for publication in Beginning Level Volumes of the *Celebrating Diversity in String Music Anthology*. His works and performances can be found on SoundCloud and Youtube.

Edwards was an officer and founding member of the University of Tennessee's Black Musicians Alliance (est. Fall 2019), a student-led organization dedicated to representing students of color and promoting underrepresented musicians. He was also a member of Phi Mu Alpha's Theta-Omicron chapter and has previously served as the social media coordinator and music director.